SCIENCE ACCORDING TO MOSES

THE FOUNDATION OF A BIBLICAL WORLD VIEW

Volume I

G. THOMAS SHARP

Creation Truth Publicaitons
P.O. Box 1435
Noble, OK 73068
(405) 872-9856

SCIENCE ACCORDING TO MOSES
THE FOUNDATION OF A BIBLICAL WORLD VIEW

♦

VOLUME I

♦

Copyright © 1992

Creation Truth Publications, Inc.
P. O. Box 1435
Noble, Oklahoma 73068

First Edition 1992
Second Edition 1996

ISBN 0-9634981-2-6 (Second Edition)
Library of Congress Catalog Card No. 96-085524 (Second Edition)
ISBN 0-9634981-0-X (First Edition)
Library of Congress Catalog Card No. 92-74832 (First Edition)
History, Philosophy, Religion
Printed in the United States of America

ALL RIGHTS RESERVED

No part of this book may be reproduced in any manner whatsoever without written permission from the publisher, except in the case of brief quotations for articles, reviews, or for teaching purposes. For additional copies of this book, or to arrange seminars covering the material in this book, write to: Creation Truth Foundation, Inc., P.O. Box 1435, Noble, OK 73068, or call (800) 554-9049 or FAX (405) 872-7500.

This book has also been translated and published in Russian and Spanish and will soon be available in French.

Printed by A.A. of L. Printing Co., South Houston, Texas. Line art by Mrs. Cynthia Reed Morris. Chapter title graphics by Troy Matthews' Graphics, Oklahoma City, Oklahoma. Photos provided by TSE

Lovingly dedicated to my dearest friend and earthly father,

George Thomas Sharp, Sr., 1920-1976.

His careful oversight and godly example remains in my heart to this very day.

                G.T.S.
                October 18, 1992

Contents

Foreword (Second Edition) i

Foreword (First Edition) iii

Acknowledgements (Second Edition) vi

Acknowledgements (First Edition) vii

Prologue x

1. World View: The God That Governs 1
   - ◇ Overview 3
   - ◇ Case in Point 4
   - ◇ The Ruling Paradigm 5
   - ◇ America's Original Paradigm 7
   - ◇ An Incredible Paradigm Shift 10
   - ◇ The Ultimate Objective of a World View . . . 18

2. Mixture: The Curse of the Fall 27
   - ◇ Overview 28
   - ◇ Man's Original Estate 30
   - ◇ Man's Greatest Task 32
   - ◇ Darwinism's Chief Implication 37
   - ◇ Darwinistic Science 40
   - ◇ America: Her Purpose 44
   - ◇ Evolutionary Mixture in Evangelicalism 51
   - ◇ Selfism: The Peril of Modern Evolutionism . 56
   - ◇ Self Help: Does it Really Help? 59
   - ◇ Counseling Mania 63
   - ◇ Beatitudinal vs. Attitudinal Holiness 72

3. What Is Real Knowledge? 81
   - ◇ Overview 82
   - ◇ How Does Man Choose Knowledge 84

◇ The Inseparable Relationship of Knowledge
and World View 88
◇ The Founders of Modern Science Were
Creationists 95
◇ The Knowledge Base Shift was
Not Scientific 98
◇ The Knowledge Change Begins 102
◇ The Renaissance and the Rise of
Modern Science 105
◇ The Greek Basis for the Shift 108
◇ Heliocentric View vs. Geocentric View ... 115
◇ The Censorship of Real History 120
◇ The Renaissance: A Deeper Look 127
◇ The Renaissance and Aristotle 130
◇ A Little About the Reformation 135
◇ The Congealing Force of
the Enlightenment 142
◇ Evolutionism: Our Present World View ... 146
◇ Summary 150

RESOURCE NOTES 155

BIBLIOGRAPHY 179

APPENDIXES
    A. Creation Scientists 197
    B. Necessity for Design
       (a letter written by Dr. Wernher von Braun
       of NASA, father of our space program, to
       the California State Board of Education). ... 200
    C. Sources of Creation Materials 203

INDEX 207

Please Note: This is book 1 of 3. The pagination of this series reflects the continous nature of the content.

FOREWORD
(SECOND EDITION)

Having read the first edition of Tom Sharp's fascinating book ***Science According to Moses***, with real appreciation, I am happy to write this Foreword to his second edition. As a historian and educator, with many years of study and experience, Dr. Sharp has developed a keen understanding of the historical trends in our nation, which have led to our present religious, social and moral decadence.

The underlying cause of our nation's decline from its solid Biblical foundations to what many have called a post-Christian (or even anti-Christian) society has been its acceptance of evolutionary scientism, not only in the schools and colleges, but also in practically all our institutions—even most of the "mainline" (as well as new-age) churches. This truth is not widely understood; but it is a factual reality, and Dr. Sharp has provided thorough documentation, along with his own very insightful analysis, to demonstrate it.

Naturally, he is greatly concerned about this, as many of us are, and his book constitutes an urgent call to those in his own denomination and to all Americans to come back to God and to a fully Biblical, Christian, creationist faith before it's too late.

I heartily endorse the emphases and conclusions of this significant book and would encourage all concerned people of good will to read it, to appropriate its perspective into their own world view, and then to live and witness as God has commanded us in His Word. It could make a difference.

> Henry M. Morris, Ph.D.
> Founder and President Emeritus
> Institute for Creation Research
> El Cajon, California

FOREWORD
(First Edition)

In his speech accepting renomination for the Presidency on June 27, 1936, Franklin D. Roosevelt said; "THIS GENERATION OF AMERICANS HAVE A RENDEZVOUS WITH DESTINY." I believe that the Church of the 1990's has a "RENDEZVOUS WITH DESTINY." That "destiny," if the present church can fulfill it, will begin with the process of reversing the trend of the total secularization of our culture and society. Before we can begin that process, however, we must recognize the great tragedy of that secularization, and its "root" cause.

I believe that ALL contemporary ethical problems are the result of this secularization. These problems include abortion, infanticide, euthanasia, addiction, poverty, racial prejudice, perverse sexual orientations, as well as unethical business practices including usury. The elimination of the Bible as a standard for ethics and morality has resulted in a pluralistic society without moral absolutes. The fact that God established on Sinai what is right and what is wrong is foreign to our contemporary culture.

We ask ourselves, "How did this happen?" Though there are many contributing factors to this secularization process, the foundation for this process was built upon the publication of Charles Darwin's famous book: *The Origin of Species By Means of Natural Selection*. On the cover of the book *Darwin* published by W. W. Norton & Company, New York in 1970, these words were inscribed:

> *"It is impossible to overstate the impact of Charles Darwin's work on Western civilization.*

> *As much as anyone in the modern era, he changed man's thinking and his influence is still felt in virtually all aspects of our lives."*

The basic teaching of evolution, and the resultant "Darwinian anthropology," is in direct contrast to the Biblical view of man. The Bible sees man not only as "created by God" but "made in the image of God." This view gives each man individual dignity, destiny, and purpose. Take away creation and you make man simply another "rational animal."

Contemporary secular thinking is predicated on the premise that man is nothing more than a "rational animal." No wonder we can "abort babies" without offending our conscience. No wonder we can think about euthanasia for our senior citizens. The very premise of the "survival of the fittest" is repulsive to one who believes the Scripture. Yet our whole secular society has embraced this premise. Thus we can make the "survival" of the mother to be far more important than the "survival" of the infant. It has been said that even the industrial revolution with its attendant dehumanization of the worker was a result of Darwin's theory of "the survival of the fittest."

The tragedy of this "secularization" of our minds extends further than the persons outside the church. The church itself has also experienced the devastating effects of this false premise. We can trace the beginning of this "trend" toward the "secularization" of Christian thought to the teachings of Aristotle and the affect he had upon St. Thomas Aquinas. These men introduced the "idea" that "all truth can be apprehended by the five senses." This "blending" of secular thought with Christian thought set the stage for the church to accept the atheistic idea that physical matter is the only true reality, and as such is the source of all physical phenomenon.

Through Aristotle and Aquinas the church was "set up" to at least partially embrace the "new" ideas of Darwin's theory, and the supremacy of the material universe. The church itself, even including Evangelicalism, has embraced a new world view partially predicated on a mixture of Biblical Theism and Darwinian Evolution.

Revival in this last decade of the 20th century must be more than Evangelists conducting major crusades. A genuine 1990's revival must bring about a complete revolution in the thinking of the Church, which will affect the thinking of the world. It is imperative that the church understand the "problem" so that we may adequately address the major issues of our society today.

I will go so far as to state that all of our sociological problems in contemporary society are a result of a new world view framed by Darwin. If we are going to reverse this trend we must establish the proper foundation for the building of a Biblical world view based on the first chapters of the book of Genesis.

G. Thomas Sharp will serve the church in his generation well, if they will "listen" to the prophetic word that God has given through his teaching and writings. *Science According to Moses* is more than another book against evolution, or about creationism, it is a PROPHETIC WORD TO THE CHURCH! Let us read it, for contained between these pages is the "blueprint" for our "RENDEZVOUS WITH DESTINY."

Thomas F. Reid, D.D.
Pastor of The Tabernacle
Orchard Park, New York

Acknowledgements
(Second Edition)

The editing and revision of this book in preparation for the printing of the second edition was overwhelming and could not have been accomplished without the help and assistance of a host of technical specialists. I especially want to thank Mr. Ian Taylor, President of the Bible Science Association (Zimmerman, MN), who both read the text and made many valuable suggestions as well as helped in the obtaining of the photography.

I am indeed grateful to Dr. John Morris, President of the Institute for Creation Research (El Cajon, CA), for reading the text and providing the endorsement for the back cover. Also, I must thank Dr. Henry M. Morris, who I believe to be the father of the modern creationist revival in America, and who also is the Founder and President Emeritus of ICR (El Cajon, CA), for his sensitive review and foreword.

There were many others who assisted me in this task. I must mention the following: Dr. Steve Deckard, Dr. David Barton, Dr. Haskell Rycroft, Pastor Louis W. Osborne, Jr. and Dr. Jack Foree—Thank-you!

For the untiring labor of Mrs. Dee London of Waterloo, IL, who faithfully and painstakingly did all of the computer work on the manuscript, I am extremely thankful. Again, I must thank my loving wife for her patient support and prayerful encouragement. However—ultimately—**TO GOD BE THE GLORY!**

G. Thomas Sharp
1996

ACKNOWLEDGEMENTS
(First Edition)

The preparation and completion of a book of this scope could have never been fully realized without the foregoing labor of a multitude of authors, researchers, and teachers. It would be impossible to give all of them their due recognition in this small space. However, as in any written project of this kind, there is always a special group of individuals who are essential to the finalization of that undertaking—so it is with this volume! Accordingly, I would like to gratefully acknowledge them at this time.

I want to especially thank Dr. Thomas F. Reid, pastor of The Tabernacle (Orchard Park, New York), who is also a well-known television and conference speaker, for reading the manuscript and writing the Foreword.

Not only so, there were a number of other key individuals, who made this project a reality. There were scientists, Bible scholars, and grammatical advisors, who reviewed the manuscript and made many helpful recommendations, for which I am indeed deeply appreciative. They were:

Edward F. Blick, Ph.D., Professor of Aerospace, Mechanical and Nuclear Engineering, University of Oklahoma.

Roger Rusk, M.S., Professor Emeritus of Physics, University of Tennessee.

George Thompson, M.S., English and Mathematics, Bridge Creek High School, Blanchard, Oklahoma.

Haskell Rycroft, D.D., Pastor of Rays of Life Church, Lexington, Oklahoma.

Debbie Bailey, M.S., Elementary and Secondary Education, Norman, Oklahoma.

CheriLyn Smith, B.A., Public Relations and Journalism, Noble, Oklahoma.

Leslie Woodard, B.S., Mathematics and Computer Science, Norman, Oklahoma.

In addition, I am deeply indebted to the help given to this project by both Pastor and Mrs. Jimmy Greer as well as Pastor and Mrs. Larry Holland and the Abundant Life Fellowship, Memphis, Tennessee. Moreover, I must give my deep-felt thanks to Mr. Jim Seals, whose technical advice and assistance in computer programming and operations were invaluable.

To Dr. Henry M. Morris, President and Founder of the Institute for Christian Research (El Cajon, California), who selflessly permitted me to use and reproduce his materials, and who also gave me much needed technical advice regarding this publication, I give my heartfelt thanks. I am also extremely grateful to David Barton, President of WallBuilders, Inc., for his permission to quote from his masterful book *The Myth of Separation*. I must further mention TFE Publishing and author Ian Taylor (Toronto, Ontario), for granting permission to quote from his outstanding work, *In The Minds of Men*.

An important link to the success of this work, without which it could have never materialized, was the patient oversight of Mr. Keith Ferguson (Memphis, Tennessee). Keith directed the printing of this volume—THANKS Keith! The long hours and prayerful creativity of Mrs. Cynde Morris—the artist—are truly appreciated.

Furthermore, I must thank Dena Johnson, a senior and presidential scholar at Oklahoma Baptist University, who helpfully read the manuscript. Ben and Ginger Silvia, dear friends, their prayer and review of the manuscript was also truly helpful. There was also mom, Mrs. Ruth Sharp, who read and reread the manuscript many times; as well as Mrs. Annabelle Pastore, my second mother, whose prayer and spiritual support were incalculable. I must mention the loving patience and understanding of my sons Thomas, Timothy, and Theron, and my precious daughter Tammera. Finally, other than the Lord Jesus Christ, the two most important people contributing to the completion of this work were: Edward J. Kelley, D.D., pastor of Christian Life Center, a faithful congregation of believers (Birmingham, Alabama)—my father in the gospel—and spiritual mentor. THANK YOU, Bro. Kelley! Finally, and most importantly, I thank Mrs. Diane Fay Sharp, my devoted wife of 29 years, whose nimble fingers typed and retyped the manuscript—hours and hours. I am deeply indebted to this godly lady! **TO GOD BE THE GLORY!**

G. Thomas Sharp
1992

PROLOGUE

The wise man accurately declared, "...of making many books there is no end..." (Ecclesiastes 12:12). The preparation of this series of short volumes (of which this is the first), would be totally unnecessary if they were just another study of the rightness or wrongness of the evolutionary theory. God has raised in our century illimitable understanding concerning the scientific and historical truthfulness of His Word.* Therefore, to simply show the scientific poverty of evolutionary theory is not the intent of this book. However, within the fallout produced by the modern scientific revolution (1600 to present), there are several eminent dangers to the Christian believer that have settled comfortably within our Western culture. Dr. Wilder-Smith said it this way:

> *In the wake of the application of the so-called scientific method, a monoculture** of technical know-how has developed and is spread-*

---

*Men like Henry M. Morris, Ph.D., Director of the Institute for Creation Research, El Cajon, California; Gary Parker, Ed.D., Clearwater Christian College, Clearwater, Florida; Thomas G. Barnes, D. Sc., Professor Emeritus of Physics, University of Texas, at El Paso, Texas; Edward Blick, Ph.D., Professor of Petroleum Engineering, University of Oklahoma, Norman, Oklahoma; Larry Butler, Ph.D., Professor of Biochemistry, Purdue University, West Lafayette, Indiana; Duane T. Gish, Ph.D., Associate Director, Institute for Creation Research, El Cajon, California; Harold S. Slusher, Ph.D., Professor of Planetary Sciences, University of Texas, at El Paso, Texas; John C. Whitcomb, Jr., Th.D., Director of Post-Graduate Studies, Grace Theological Seminary, Winona Lake, Indiana; A. E. Wilder- Smith, D. Sc., Ph.D., Dr. es. Sc., F.R.I.C.; and scores of others have been utilized by the Holy Spirit to overwhelmingly confirm the scientific and historical accuracy of God's Holy Word.

**Monoculture—Dr. Wilder-Smith is using this term to show that as far as most scientists are concerned the scientific method is the only valid method for the discovery and development of real knowledge.

*ing rapidly around the globe. Knowing how to tackle a problem by the scientific approach is not, however, the only ingredient of the present scientific monoculture. A philosophy of life accompanies this technical ability. Science studies matter and is not very good at much else. And the study of matter has led many to believe that a wholly material universe is the only reality. For them, all problems and all solutions are purely material. This philosophy of life is known as **scientific materialism**. One of its branches of thought is neo-Darwinism...* [1] (emphasis added)

While the apparent scientific support for the doctrine of evolution has all but vanished, the impact from all this "scientific" stuff has left a strategically dangerous philosophical residue in our culture. Founded on scientific materialism and supported by Darwinian evolutionism, this mind-set has become our cultural world view and as such, it dominates the mind-set of most Westerners, Americans in particular.

The blackness of evolutionism and the whiteness of true Biblical Christianity have been so thoroughly mixed, in such a gradual process, and for such a long time, until even the best among the present Christian community portray a dingy gray perception of truth in both their world view and their life style. Accordingly, in this series of volumes I will not be as interested in the age of the earth, or whether man has a common ancestor, or the extent of Noah's flood, etc., as I will be in the presentation of data that cogently shows the origin, the extent of encroachment, and the present predicament in which the Western culture finds itself as the result of evolutionism, and especially how all of this has affected the church.

THE NEED FOR THIS VOLUME

I have been a gospel minister since 1961 and a certified school teacher since 1964. From that time I have pastored a church, held hundreds of revival meetings, youth camps, seminars, etc., and taught school (both private and public), in three states. Early in my professional experience (mid-1960's), it became obvious to me that something deep and foreboding had attacked our American culture. As it turned out, I wasn't aware just how deep and foreboding the attack really was. At the time, I felt that this condition was due simply to a youth-centered counter cultural rebellion and would pass with their maturity. Without understanding its motive or its origin, I geared up to preach harder against what my denomination dubbed "sin," and doubled my efforts to hold up a "standard" (these expressions I later learned were just distinctives of my denomination), thinking that in this way I could help the parents and their young people through this crisis.

To my chagrin, however, in the early 1970's I became acquainted with a study done in Tennessee. This survey reported that among the evangelical churches sampled, they were losing 75% of their young people by age 15. The church I was pastoring was also experiencing this same devastating phenomenon. Ostensibly, this condition was not a surface issue or a social trend that would soon pass away as I formerly thought. It was something broad and far-reaching, and was bent on the total destruction of our Hebrew-Christian tradition.*

---

*The term "Judaism" possesses a dichotomy of meaning, and because of the nature of modern political zionism, it may not be the best designation for Old Testament religion. As a matter of fact, I recently heard Professor Roger Rusk quote a Chief Rabbi of America, Stephan S. Wise, as saying: *"The return from Babylon, and the adoption of the Babylonian Talmud, marks the end of Hebraism and the beginning of Judaism."* As such, Christian orthodoxy cannot properly be aligned with modern Judaism. In other words, the rabbi-synagogue-Talmud system, (Modern Judaism), is not commensurate with the priest-temple-Moses system, (Old Testament Hebrew religion). Accordingly, to link our heritage with the Old Testament and its JHVH-Elohim, (Redeeming Creator), it is much more accurate to say Hebrew-Christian rather than Judeo-Christian. By this term, (Hebrew-Christian), we bypass the corruption of modern Judaism, Zionism, and the like, and properly connect with the God and saints of the Old Testament. This is not to say the word Judah, or the word Jew, is not a proper Biblical designation. They are! But, modern Judaism, Zionism, etc., carries with it some anti-Scriptural connotations, and as such I have chosen to use the phrase Hebrew-Christian. Moreover, you will notice several authors quoted in this volume have used the expression "Judeo-Christian" in their writing. Ostensibly, they refer by this expression to the priest-temple-Mosaic system. Their use of the phrase, like the term Jew, is intended to refer to the people and religious faith of the Old Testament, even though it is now technically a

I had already sat, on too many occasions, across the desk from weeping parents who were seeking counsel and advice because of an acute sorrow that resulted from a wayward teenager. Some parents would report to me that it was as if their sons and daughters had become strangers in their own homes. My greatest problem, as I recall during those years, was that I really didn't have an answer, or a solution, or an explanation for the dilemma. I had done all of those churchy things in an attempt to ameliorate what I perceived to be the problem; namely revivals, vacation Bible schools, youth camps, weekly youth nights, etc. We even, in the mid-70's, opened a Christian day school, but all to no avail for an alarming number of our youth.

The sociologists and psychologists at the time said, in effect, that we were experiencing a "generation gap;" however, I later learned that the rebellion and the open rejection of Biblical authority had very little to do with the so-called baby boomer generation,* per se. The baby boomers, as a distinct population, were not any different than any other generation at any other time in our history. They were, however, uniquely trained.

There have been literally hundreds of books and articles written about this particular population of Americans. Each of which in some way have attempted to analyze, explain, or justify the curious behaviors of this group. Accordingly, you can find just about as many explanations for the rationale of the "baby boomers" as there are publications on the subject. Nevertheless, there is a thread of general agreement in the literature about this period. That is, this generation was the first generation in our

---

debatable term for their intended meaning. (See: Roger Rusk, *The Other End of the World*, (Knoxville, Tennessee: Plantation House, Inc., 1988). Anyone interested in Professor Rusk's book can order it from: Creation Truth Foundation, P. O. Box 1435, Noble, OK 73068.

*Generally the "Baby Boomer generation" is considered to be those individuals that were born in the United States between the years 1946 and 1964.

history to be controlled by a world view of "selfism" that was grounded in evolutionary materialism, relativism, and naturalism.

It became apparent to me that the crowd of the sixties, and after, were not behaving as they were because of a "generation gap." Rather, it was a cultural gap. The Evangelical Conservatives had withdrawn into their own religious cloister, and as a result, the religious liberals and the intellectual skeptics were free to openly attack the Biblical Christian base in our American society. This they did successfully! Consequently, by the time we reached the 1980's America had become totally secular and pagan. Alas, the Hebrew-Christian tradition, upon which our great country was founded, had been totally eclipsed.

The Cultural Change And The Church

Our Lord prayed that, while we should not be taken out of the world, that we must be kept from the evil that controls the world's system (John 17:15). It is apparent that the idea contained in the Lord's use of the word "evil" is tantamount to our modern expression "world view." In other words, whereas the law of God is the world view that controls the kingdom of God, the kingdom of Satan is ruled by iniquity (or no law). Since these two points of view are complete opposites, as well as being basic to one's choice of values and lifestyle (i.e. values and lifestyle dictated by iniquity or no-law versus values and lifestyle emanating from righteousness or law), it becomes the chief function of the church and Christian ministry to train disciples to see and live life from God's point of view. Thus world view transformation is the principal task of the believer, and the primary reason for God giving ministerial gifts to the Church (Ephesians 4:7-12; Luke 8:4-16). The following Scriptural expressions are all aspects of this truth:

1. My sheep hear my voice...and they FOLLOW Me.... (John 10:9).
2. We ought to OBEY God rather than men (Acts 5:29).
3. ...he also did predestinate [us] to be CONFORMED to the IMAGE of his Son...(Romans 8:29).
4. And be not CONFORMED to this world; but be ye TRANSFORMED by the RENEWING OF YOUR MIND...(Romans 12:2).
5. ...Know ye not that a little LEAVEN LEAVENETH the whole lump? (I Corinthians 5:6).
6. For the weapons of our warfare are not carnal, but mighty through God to the PULLING DOWN OF STRONGHOLDS; CASTING DOWN IMAGINATIONS, and every HIGH THING that exalteth itself against the knowledge of God...
(II Corinthians 10:4-5).
7. That ye put OFF concerning the former manner of life, the old man...And be RENEWED IN YOUR MIND; and PUT ON THE NEW MAN...(Ephesians 4:22-24).
8. Let this MIND be in you, which was also in Christ Jesus...(Philippians 2:5).
9. And have put ON the new man, which is RENEWED IN KNOWLEDGE after the IMAGE of Him that CREATED HIM (Colossians 3:10).
10. And the very God of peace SANCTIFY you WHOLLY... (I Thessalonians 5:23).
11. ...and EXERCISE thyself rather unto GODLINESS (I Timothy 4:7).
12. ...And let every one that nameth the name of Christ DEPART FROM INIQUITY (II Timothy 2:19).
13. ...let us lay aside every weight and the sin which DOTH SO EASILY BESET US...(Hebrews 12:1).
14. ...Be ye HOLY; for I am HOLY (I Peter 1:16).

15. He that saith, I know him and KEEPETH not his commandments, is a liar, and the truth is not in him (I John 2:4).

The bottom line is simply this: when an individual is converted to Christ, his world view is plainly the product of his cultural conditioning, which is a process generally referred to as socialization. If, therefore, the culture is essentially Biblically Christian, the world view transitional process that must take place subsequent to conversion, is much easier. However, in America today, because our culture is no longer Hebrew-Christian, but rather pagan, this process is incredibly complicated. As a matter of fact, the tragedy of our generation is that we've lived during the time that our culture actually shifted from Hebrew-Christian to pagan. As a result, we find ourselves in the unenviable position of being products of both worlds. This deceiving mixture has caused most church groups and denominations to lose their Biblical exactness and fervor and has left America, by and large, without a clear Biblical example.

Another salient point needs to be mentioned before I go on. In the above mentioned Scriptures (which, by the way, are only a token of the scores that could have been cited), special attention needs to be given to the intensity and choice of Paul's words for world view transformation to those believers converted from the Greek world. Of all the world's cultures, this one seems above all most dangerous to Biblical Christian thought. Not only is Greek thought dangerous to believers, it is above all others the most difficult to transform (Colossians 2:8). In this connection, we will soon come to see that our present American culture is a product of ancient Greece that was transported to our day via the Renaissance and the Enlightenment. In this regard, the warning Paul issued to the Colossian believers is applicable to us:

> *See to it that **no one takes you captive through hollow and deceptive philosophy, which depends on human tradition and the***

basic principles of this world rather than on *Christ.* (Colossians 2:8, NIV)

OUR GREATEST DANGER

Heresy and deception have always been the great peril of any age. More specifically, heresy, the fountain head from which deception flows, is nothing more or less than a genuine Biblical truth that has become unbalanced or exaggerated with regard to the total body of revelation. As you will soon come to understand by reading chapters one and two of this volume, our present Western materialistic and naturalistic view point, which developed gradually from the Renaissance until now, is the product of philosophical change that has affected policy and procedure in the Western world (also the Eastern culture), and has fatally altered the Christian foundation.

As a result, the world view conditioning that is performed by the socialization process (a natural procedure of any culture, and one from which no one is exempt), becomes the bane of the Christian Church in her attempts at being obedient to the Lord. Furthermore, this same world view orientation is a significant forestaller of the return of the glory to Zion. Built into our socialization process today, and for the past eighty or so years, there has been a thorough value's conditioning scheme that manipulates the clarification of behavioral and attitudinal standards which has stifled the development of a **pure faith** for the vast majority of the churches' disciples.

The greatest impact of our conditioning process, and a factor difficult to overcome, is that the essentials of one's world view are developed early in one's life. It is a well-known fact that most of an individual's personality, values, moral foundation, and even one's intelligence potential is developed in the years before puberty. Dr. A. E. Wilder-Smith posits that after puberty "the plasticity of the mind in dealing with new facts and theories can become impaired."[2] As a matter of fact, Dr. Smith said recently in a lecture regarding the relationship between heredity and environment in our development, that the environment before puberty is a vital factor. Environment, he said, can be either positive or negative in the achievement of one's genetic potential in such areas as I.Q., brain development, etc. In other words, early in their life, our sons and daughters must both explicitly see and plainly hear Biblical Christian training.

TEACHING V. TRAINING

The fact that the terms *teaching* and *training* can be displayed in contradistinction as in this heading—a legitimate reality today—is indicative of a serious breakdown in our present understanding of the Biblical educational processes. The Hebrew-Christian tradition clearly shows that "to teach" is "to train." However this is not the case in today's world either at home, at school, or in church.

Any contradiction between the curricular content* (what we write and speak), and our example of pure Biblical-Christian values (what we are), deposits in our students seeds of unbelief and rebellion against God their Creator. Thus eradicating the purpose for education in the first place—the perpetuation of the Biblical Christian world view! Specifically, and even more disconcerting, any disagreement that exists between what is being taught in the written curriculum either at home, school, or at church and the lifestyle behaviors of the one doing the teaching

---

*Much can be said about the relationship and importance between the written and the unwritten curriculum. The written curriculum being the Bible, textbooks, Sunday School literature, etc. The unwritten curriculum being our everyday lifestyle, our interactions with others, and personal behaviors and attitudes. Suffice it to say that what we are trains our sons and daughters more efficiently than what we say. That is, we teach more effectively by our own lifestyle and personal values than anything we may say in a classroom setting.

ultimately destroys the developmental intention of the written content. This is especially true of training for value and morality growth and development. Sadly, the modern church is guilty of these heterodox educational practices. Why?

Of the many Scriptural passages that treat the true function and purpose of education, Deuteronomy 6:4-8 and Proverbs 22:6 are among the best. I want to quickly appeal to both of them in answering the question "WHY?" mentioned above.

Deuteronomy 6:4-8 records the greatest commandment of holy Scripture. Simply stated, Moses declared that Jehovah, our Elohim, is One, and that our chief duty to Him is to love Him with all our heart, soul, mind, and strength. As a vital part of our love to Him, we are not only to pursue a life of unmixed devotion and service to Him and His cause, but we also are to instill this same world view in our sons and daughters. Moses said (verses 6 and 7):

> *These commandments that I give you today are to be upon your hearts. Impress them on your children. Talk about them when you sit at home and when you walk along the road, when you lie down and when you get up.* (NIV)

Four times each day fathers and mothers are to disseminate godly principles into their sons and daughters. In other words, the love of the Creator dictates a way of life. Its not a religion made up of human creeds and conduct, but it is a relationship with the living God who Created us and also gave Himself as a ransom for our redemption. Anything, therefore, that would hinder this process—both our development of this world view and its instillment in our sons and daughters—also violates this great commandment.

PROLOGUE

To the latter, Solomon wrote in Proverbs 22:6 that parents are to "***train*** up a child in the way he should go..." What does it mean "to train up a child in the way he should go"? How do the specific terms teaching and training correspond with this Biblical statement?

The word *"train"* is only used three times in the Old Testament (King James Version), and in each instance it is translated from a different Hebrew word. In this case, the word "train" is *chanak* (pronounced khaw-nak'). This word has a unique derivation. The margin of most Bibles will indicate that this word could also be translated "catechize," meaning daily, systematic instruction in Biblical dogma and its application in daily affairs.

Dr. Francis Brown, et al., gives the following comment about this word as it is used in Proverbs 22:6. He writes that to train is "[to] rub [the] palate of [a] child with chewed dates."[3] In practice this meant that during the weaning process a Hebrew mother would chew some solid food (dates), and then she would place this masticated food into her young child's mouth by using an eating utensil, or with her finger. In this process, she would touch the child's palate which is deep in the mouth. When the palate is touched, an automatic swallowing response is set off and the unsuspecting child swallows the new food immediately. Thus after repeated feedings, the infant establishes a taste for different kinds of food.

Simply stated, Solomon is teaching that parents are the exclusive instruments in developing godly values and behaviors in their children. To "train" a child, parents must touch their son's or daughter's mental "palate" with proper lifestyle habits in a consistent systematic process prior to puberty. In other words, we are to form in them a Christian world view by convincing their heart with truth through teaching (the written curriculum), and the practical application of teaching (the unwritten curriculum). To teach and to demonstrate the reality of our oral tradition in life equals Biblical training. However, to teach and then to abandon our own teaching by departures in our lifestyle also trains our sons and daughters. It trains them to ignore our teaching!

The tragic irony presently emanating from this fact is that even though we have energetically taught doctrines and creeds to our children through scores of church related programs (most of them being Biblical), we did not realize that our own world view and lifestyle was contradictory to the Biblical principles contained in our own teaching. As a result, we taught Biblical truth to some degree, but indeed we were training our own children to view the world from a completely different mind-set as that espoused by the Bible. What we failed to do was to first love the Lord, our God, with all of our hearts. Thus clearly demonstrating to our sons and daughters the reality of our teaching. As a result of our failure in this regard, we have been training our children to ignore Biblical teaching, because it obviously was not important enough for our own devotion and commitment.

The organized church didn't help much in this matter at all. They (leadership and all), were so busy doing those churchy kinds of things—building buildings, organizing new programs, competing with the church across the street, etc.—until the message of Christ was lost in the dust of religious activity. To use the words of the late Vance Havner: *"The church has been so busy doing the work of the Lord until she has forgotten the Lord of the work."* Religious busyness is the trademark of the modern church, and this is especially true of the Evangelicals. Teaching our denominational tenets has become a part of this busyness. After all, being a good Baptist, or a good Methodist, or a good Presbyterian, or a good Pentecostal, etc., is the uppermost religious task of the ministry! So we are, indeed, teaching! Alas, our teaching, along with all of our other religious activities, has not offset the fact that both the culture and ourselves have become pagan.

To "teach" simply means the impartation of information, unless it is delivered in context of tutelage and mentorship (e.g. Moses and Joshua, Paul and Timothy, Elijah and Elisha, or Jesus and the eleven). For teaching to produce training, the instructor must not only speak right words, his words must also be a description of his own world and life view. What we failed to ascertain is that, during the first sixty years of this century, our own American culture gradually became more and more pagan—the result of evolutionary takeover. As such, a God defying mind-set gradually replaced the true Biblical world view among professing believers. At best, therefore, the church community became just a reflection of the greater culture. So, while we professed allegiance to Biblical truth, our world view and lifestyle betrayed our claims. Our teaching, therefore, did not effect training in our own sons and daughters.

The so-called "baby boomers" (the sixties generation—many of them the sons and daughters of church members), saw this discrepancy immediately, because our real values were heard much more than our words. In effect, therefore, we helped the pagans train our own children. What a paradox! Furthermore, and just as important, Christian parents have been taking their "sons" and "daughters" to the national "palate toucher" (the public school), who have been shamelessly and persuasively touching their young formative palates with paganistic philosophy, values, and life-style for the last fifty years or so. From this dilemma, without true repentance based on Biblical truth, we are hopelessly doomed!

The reality that we must understand in all of this is that this entire pitiful scenario was accomplished in the name of science. The enemy instigated an apparently reasonable "scientific model" for the explanation of first origins that excludes the need for a Creator God. This paved the way for a total ideological rebellion. Is it any wonder that we are presently experiencing such a vast departure from Christian values in our American society? Not only so, we are even experiencing incredible moral aberrations within homes where the church and the Bible are still revered as the body of Christ and the inspired word of God, respectively. The evidence for this decay within today's church is quite easily seen, however, to display the acute nature of this problem consider the remarks of Professor Dewey Bertolini.

EVIDENCE OF DECAY

In 1989, Professor Dewey Bertolini* made these extremely salient comments while speaking on the topic, *Youth Trends In The 21st Century*. In the midst of his presentation, Bertolini read from and commented on a local California newspaper article that had been distributed in the fall of 1989. He said that the article discussed the results of a:

> *California Panel on Public School Curriculum that voted unanimously (12-0) for the teaching of evolution as a scientific fact. The same article said that the panel also, 12-0 voted to ban the teaching of divine creation theories in science classes. Do you understand what's going on? We [the church community] have not yielded turf by acres, we have yielded turf by the millimeter. This [shift in world view] has been a subtle, gradual erosion. The article continues by quoting the California Assistant State Superintendent of Public Instruction, who said," The whole thing is a side-show. Come on! How many people really believe the world is only 6000 years old? The issue is*

---

*Professor Bertolini teaches at Master's College, a four year liberal arts Christian college in the state of California. He made the above statements while speaking to a workshop session of the International Fellowship of Christian School Administrators. The meeting was sponsored by the Association of Christian Schools International, which is the largest professional Christian school organization in America.

*not whether the world was created in six days. The issue is whether our science classes are going to be teaching **science**,* as much science as possible and only science. Now, what are the practical ramifications of this?* [4] (emphasis added)

Bertolini, while answering the question posed by this California Education official, tells of a recent outing that he and his family took at a local restaurant in their hometown. While he and his family were eating, four junior high school students walked into the restaurant and were seated just behind his family. He said they were wearing tee-shirts that displayed blatant profanity as well as the rest of the usual trappings that clearly represents a pagan culture. He said he plainly over-heard them planning their sexual exploits for that evening following the ball game. Bertolini then made a very revealing statement:

*Just ten years ago, if I would have talked to junior high kids like these, I would have approached this same scene on the basis of rebellion. I would have talked to them from the standpoint of their behavior being rebellious. I would have prefaced my remarks to them by saying, "You know what's right and you have chosen to rebel." But, today if I would talk to young people as these, I would not identify them as rebellious. They are **not** rebelling! **They are living in obedience to the ethic they have been taught as right.*** [5] (emphasis added)

---

*This California educational official is obviously defining the word "science" as being interchangeable with the phrase "Darwinian evolution."

Bertolini said coming to this understanding was difficult and slow but was expedited by an experience he had in 1987 while teaching at Master's College. Now remember, Master's College is a Christian evangelical college where tuition is far above normal and where policies are very conservative. Because of this, Bertolini said he assumed that the student body should be the cream of the "evangelical" crop. While this is probably true, he said to his surprise:

> *When questioned about immorality and other issues, they [many of the members of the new freshman class at Master's College] felt no guilt about it at all. This simply does not compute! How can someone who names the name of Christ engage in an act so obviously an aberration from Biblical morality, and then*

Figure **P-a**. Charles Darwin was so revered in England that the British Museum of Natural History had this statue of him placed in a prominent section of the museum. Thomas Henry Huxley is making this dedication.

tell me that they have no semblance of guilt about it at all? But, that's what they told me. Why? Because they have grown up in an environment in which God has been systematically, subtly, and strategically removed from their thinking. **They honestly do not know the difference!** *They think they are living a normal, natural, proper lifestyle. We have on our hands for the first time in the history of our country a totally secularized generation of young people.* [6] (emphasis added)

Additional evidence of this decay can be seen in the pithy remarks of Charles Colson:

Many believe that religious values and liberties have fallen victim to some sinister conspiracy in which the ACLU, humanist educators, and the media meet in darkened corridors of CBS headquarters to plot the demise of religion in America.

Admittedly, the ACLU has a powerful lobby, the media are unsympathetic, and skeptics dominate college campuses. But even if such forces were organized to consciously eradicate religious values they could do little to wipe out real Christianity.

Christian values are in retreat in the west today, primarily, I believe, because of the church itself. *If Christianity has failed to stem the rising tides of relativism it is because the church in many instances has lost the convicting force of the gospel message. Earlier we argued that while humanists did not under-*

stand humans, Christians did not understand Christianity." [7] (emphasis added)

It is now a matter of record, the Hebrew-Christian influence is no longer vital to the trends and values that are considered important in our American socialization process. As Isaiah indicated in his third chapter, a decaying society can, and most often does, have an adverse affect upon the behavior and values of God's people.

EVOLUTIONISM: OUR NEW WORLD VIEW

Obviously, then, it has now become necessary for the "watchmen on the wall" to conduct a wholesale investigation to see if "the beams of our house are **still** cedar" (Song of Solomon 1:17). It is quite possible that even the most pious among us are driven by a value system that is uniquely non-Christian. It would certainly be revealing to anyone who identifies with the American church scene if they would take the time to genuinely compare their world view with the world view presented in the Holy Scripture. The shocking reality in all of this is the fact that the only ones who are fooled by their religious profession are the vast majority of the American "Christians." You see, most present day Christian advocates are impulsive, non-doctrinal, non-foundational, experiential, and generally void of Biblical discipline, resolve, and commitment.

To accomplish this demented spiritual state of affairs, the enemy of God's kingdom has obviously summoned his most exalted strategy. The nature of this "last days" attack has been so gradual and subtle that even the holiest and wisest of the church did not connect the seemingly harmless causes with the present ruinous, even satanic, effects (see Figure **P-b**). Now it is undeniably clear; Satan has inculcated deep within our American mind-set a hideous leaven that has nearly leavened the whole lump. His attack has been nothing new, and the church should have at once perceived his clandestine plan. You can read of it in Genesis 3:1-6. This passage lucidly speaks of the age-old demonic conspiracy that has been used to overthrow God's purpose in the earth for time immemorial, i.e. the humanization of God and the deification of man. However, as in other times, we did not perceive the changing of our cultural world view to be dangerous at all. We simply adjusted our theology and went on. You can call this present phenomenon secular humanism; you can call it evolutionary materialism, or even paganism, or whatever you like! However, it is nothing short of the Mystery of Iniquity all dressed up in scientific clothes (II Thessalonians 2:7).

While the methods Satan has used to accomplish the present deception are multi-faceted (said methods I will discuss in this volume as well as those to follow), he presently supports this deception with a well-communicated massive educational scheme. The foundation for this scheme was culminated in 1859 with the first publication of Charles Darwin's famous book, *The Origin of Species By Means of Natural Selection*. The repercussions of Darwin's work are accurately described by the comments of the following academic professionals:

> In 1972, the renowned zoologist from Harvard, Ernst Mayr, indicated that evolution was *"perhaps the most fundamental of all intellectual revolutions in the history of mankind."* [8]

> In his biography of Charles Darwin, author James Moore remarked, *"More than any modern thinker—even Freud or Marx...[Darwin] has transformed the way we see ourselves on the planet."* [9]

> Theodosius Dobzhansky, about whom it was remarked at his eulogy (1975), that he was the lead-

ing evolutionist of the twentieth century, wrote that Darwin's book *The Origin of Species* "*marked a turning point in the intellectual history of mankind...[and] ushered in a new understanding of man and his place in the universe.*" [10]

Dr. Colin Brown, a leading theologian of this century, penned that, "*By far the most potent single factor to undermine popular belief in the existence of God in modern times is the evolutionary theory of Charles Darwin.*" [11]

Probably Newman Watts, an author and journalist from London, said it best—shocking, but nonetheless true! He revealed the following observation: "*In compiling my book,* Britain Without God, *I had to read a great deal of anti-religious liter-*

Figure P-b. Questions of this kind lead to doubt and doubt destroys the believer's faith.

ature. Two things impressed me. One was the tremendous amount of this literature available, and the other was the fact that every attack on the Christian faith made today has, as its basis, the doctrine of evolution." [12]

I am convinced that Darwin's feat, the popularization of the notions of atheistic evolutionism, has provided the support system whereby Satan has deepened his strangulation hold upon the faith of believers in this century. So, by the turn of the twentieth century riding on the crest of Enlightenment philosophy and strengthened by its apparent association with the genuine scientific accomplishments of the Industrial Revolution, Darwinian evolutionism became the world view for the intellectuals and college set of the entire Western World by the early 1900's. Thus the world, life, and man came to be explained and understood on the basis of evolution and evolutionary processes in all American universities and colleges.

It's not that evolution is scientifically factual, because it isn't as we shall see in the balance of these volumes, but the doctrine of evolution—nothing more than a philosophical scheme* for a godless explanation of the past—perfected the infidelity begun in the Renaissance. As a result, the Biblical idea that a supernatural Creator created the Universe and all that is in it was, therefore, discredited among the intelligentsia of both Europe and America.

To make matters worse, along with the rise of the modern scientific era came the popular idea that good knowledge can only be determined by scientific processes. Since modern science

---

*Beverly Halstead, "Popper: Good Philosophy, Bad Science?" *New Science 87*, (July 17, 1980: 215-217). In this article, Halstead quoted from Popper's autobiography *Unended Quest*: *"I have come to the conclusion that Darwinism is not a scientific theory, but a metaphysical research programma.."* (p. 215). Karl Popper is considered by many leading scientists to be the greatest philosopher of science that has ever lived.

Figure P-c. Francis Bacon (1561-1626), is often called the father of the modern scientific method because of his belief in experimentation and induction from the data. He strongly opposed Aristotle's deductive methods for acquiring scientific knowledge. A strong Bible believer, he wrote: *"There are two books laid before us to study, to prevent our falling into error; first, the volume of Scriptures, which reveal the will of God; then the volume of the Creation, which express His power."*

advocates only a sensory basis, called empirical investigation, as its guide for the achievement of knowledge and rejects the possibility of there being any lasting benefit from knowledge gained in any other way; the Bible, and its God, as the basis for understanding and learning was gradually rejected as a valid source for knowledge. This materialistic foundation became the vogue of the entire scientific community by the mid 1800's and precipitated the change of their paradigm from a creationist world view to the Darwinian point of view. The significance of this paradigm shift is explained by Samuel Morison and Henry Commager:*

> *From the year 1859, when Darwin published his* Origin of Species, *we can date a revolution not only in natural science but in thought. The new doctrine was accepted much more quickly on this side of the Atlantic than in Europe, just as inventions and technological advances were more promptly applied here. The leaders of practically every Christian sect except the Unitarians and Catholics fought hard for Genesis and special creation, and Louis Agassiz** attacked evolution of species on scientific grounds. But the doctrine spread rapidly through magazine articles, lectures, and the writings of popularizers, just as the doctrines of Newton in the previous century.* **And as with Newtonian physics so Darwinian evolution created a new intellectual norm.**

---

*Samuel Morison was the Jonathan Trumball Professor of American History at Harvard University, and Henry Commager was Professor of History at Columbia University. Both of these men lived and taught in the early and mid 1900's.

**Louis Agassiz (ag'uh-see)-1807 to 1873- was the son of a minister and the descendant of a Huguenot family that fled France under Louis XIV. Afterward, he moved to America and taught biological science at Harvard.

> *In 1860 almost everyone in America believed literally in the account of creation in the book of Genesis, and supposed that species had been created by God for man's especial benefit. By 1870 people were joking about the "missing link," and being descended from a monkey or "a protoplasmal primordial atomic globule."* **By 1900 perhaps three-fourths of the white population believed that man was merely one of the countless organisms that had evolved from the primordial slime, and that this planet was millions instead of thousands of years old**...*the important thing is that evolution and science created a new climate of opinion, and one in which we still live. It was not merely the change in man's views as to his origin on this planet that mattered.* **The implications of evolution were incorporated into every field of thought—law and history, economics and sociology, philosophy, religion, and art.** [13] (emphasis added)

One need not think that we Christians, who are living in the last decade of the twentieth century, have escaped the devastation of this philosophical mixture. The devil does not necessarily need to eradicate the Bible in order to disseminate havoc in the church. All he must do is create a little doubt in the minds of believers regarding the Creatorship of God. At this point, the rest of the Bible becomes easy prey to the skeptic's pen and accordingly the great "deceiver" has opened a Pandora's box from which all sorts of evil can flourish. The slightest question in the heart of a believer about Genesis chapters one through eleven will consciously or unconsciously render that heart vulnerable to doubt, rebellion, disobedience, and ultimately to a paganistic world view. Consequently, during the last one hundred-fifty years, the enemy has viciously attacked the first verse of the Bible, knowing that if he could cast a shroud upon that pivotal Scripture, he could implement a successful involuntary rebellion in the hearts and minds of believers with the balance of the sacred book.

SCIENCE ACCORDING TO MOSES

It is a matter of record, all Christian doctrine, practice, and action stands or falls with the strength of your faith regarding Genesis 1:1. The slightest hesitancy at this point diffuses a restraint upon the believer's foundational faith that carries into all of the Christian's life. If you are not deeply rooted upon the literal presentation of Genesis chapter one, and that without qualification and reconciliation to alternate views and special theories that have been accepted because of the supposed "facts" of modern science, you will find yourself qualifying and accommodating other extremely clear passages of Scripture to suit a modern theological point of view. Not only that, but most do not understand that to build a Christian world view one must see the world and all of life through the lenses of the first eleven chapters of Genesis. They are the world view chapters in the Scripture! Any attempt to build a Biblical world view on any other basis is not only futile but in most cases renders the world view extrabiblical or even antibiblical.

Nevertheless, today, the Christian community finds itself reading the Bible and telling God what He means in His word. This is secular humanism gone to seed! My dear friends, as sad as it is true, this is our plight today. King David lamented that if "the foundation be destroyed, what can the righteous do?" (Psalm 11:3). The "foundation has been destroyed," or at least severely damaged by the fiendish usurpation of Darwinian evolutionism, that is to say in our imaginations! Accordingly, we must have a complete restoration of the preeminent underpinning of Biblical truth concerning first origins and total reality; because total obedience, true worship, and the glorification of Christ by you and me and the entire church rests upon this restoral.

The principle verse of the entire Bible is: "In the beginning, God created the heavens and earth."* The believer who builds on this historical and Biblical foundation will always produce a lifestyle that is thoroughly Christian. You see, if we truly see God as our eternal Creator, then we will know that He is the lawgiver and that we are accountable to Him. It is, therefore, because of a lack of this understanding among evangelical Christians that I have called this series of volumes *Science According To Moses*. This title is just another way of saying that what God revealed to Moses and he (Moses) recorded in Genesis 1-11, we also can observe when we examine the world around us, and, therefore, it is the only real scientific basis for true knowledge. As such, Genesis 1-11 is the only knowledge base from which the Christian disciple can build a bona fide Biblical Christian world view.

For those who take the time to prayerfully work through the content of this book, they will see that it is my firm conviction that the Evangelical Christian community has departed from her Biblical underpinnings and is in desperate need of awakening and repentance. For awakening to come, we must first know the cause and extent of our present condition. This understanding will give us the vantage point from which to pursue a return to pure Biblical Christianity. While it is very possible that this volume may generate the need for additional study, it is nonetheless dedicated to the purpose of informing the sincere Christian disciple of the magnitude of our problem and to convince him that only as we return

---

*Dr. Henry M. Morris recently wrote that: *"The first verse of the Bible is the foundational verse of the Bible. The Book of Genesis is indeed the Bible's foundational book, and it is also obvious that the first 11 chapters of Genesis, which deal with the whole world and with all the nations, constitute the foundation for the rest of Genesis, which deals specifically with the beginnings of the nation Israel. By the same token, Chapter 1 of Genesis is the Foundational Chapter of these first 11 chapters, since it summarizes the creation of the world and all things therein. Finally, Genesis 1:1 is the foundation of all foundations and thus could be said to be the most important verse in the Bible."* Henry M. Morris, "The Most Important Verse in the Bible," *Creation Ex Nihilo* 14:2 (March-May, 1992): 20.

to and build our lives upon *Science According To Moses* can we become genuinely Christian in our world view and lifestyle. In turn, this is the only way we can bring true social reform to our land (II Chronicles 7:14).

G. Thomas Sharp
1992, 1996

CHAPTER 1

WORLD VIEW: THE GOD THAT GOVERNS

Figure **1-a**. Our perception of reality is always distorted by philosophical mixture.

OVERVIEW

"See to it that no one carries you off as spoil or makes you yourselves captive by his so-called philosophy and intellectualism, and vain deceit (idle fancies and plain nonsense), following human tradition—men's ideas of the material [rather than the spiritual] world—just crude notions following the rudimentary and elemental teachings of the universe, and disregarding [the teachings of] Christ, the Messiah."

Colossians 2:8, Amplified Version
* * * * * *

"Do you not know that if you continually surrender yourselves to any one to do his will, you are the slaves of him whom you obey, whether that be to sin, which leads to death, or to obedience which leads to righteousness?

Romans 6:16, Amplified Version
* * * * * *

"A Biblical world view gives us a clear look at reality. When we move away from that clear view, we are like children increasingly smudging a window with dirty fingerprints and then looking outside. First the colors become duller. Then the shapes begin to alter. As the dirt gets thicker, the light is progressively shut out. It becomes harder to say with accuracy what is happening out there. If this process takes place gradually, we might hardly notice what is happening but increasingly we are cut off from reality...To the extent that our world view departs from God's message to us, our perceptions are distorted..." (see Figure **1-a**)

Herbert Schlossberg & Mervin Olasky
* * * * * *

1

THE term "science" simply means *knowledge* and is derived from the Latin word *scientia*. While it is very difficult to understand the full extent of what is presently meant by the term "science," we must understand that within the recent history of science and the making of modern science there resides the answer regarding why our cultural paradigm or world view* has shifted.

CASE IN POINT

For the past few years Northeast Missouri State University has sponsored the Joseph Baldwin Academy for Eminent Young Scholars. Not long ago a brilliant young student from one of the author's biology classes was selected to attend the 1990 session of this Academy. The textbook used for this advanced placement group of young scholars was the 1987 edition of *Life: The Science of Biology*, by William K. Purves and Gordon H. Orians.

---

*The term world view will be more fully treated in Chapter 3. However this expression refers to one's fundamental belief system from which decisions are made, values are established, and priorities are arranged, etc.; it is simply one's philosophy of life. It must also be kept in mind that in a scientific, a religious, or a philosophical context, the terms paradigm, bias, preconception, and mind set are all meaningful expressions that are inherent within the connotational jurisdiction of the term world view.

After the student returned from the Academy, the author surveyed this textbook and found, on pages 18-19, one of the most revealing statements that the author has ever seen in cold print regarding the nature and influence of a world view. The straight forwardness of their remarks leaves no doubt about the important nature of one's world view. In a section entitled, **The Importance Of The World View**, Purves and Orians plainly admit that even the face of the painstaking and intricate experimentation of biological scientists, the interpretation of their findings will always be shaped according to the preconceptions that they believed prior to their experimentation. These predispositions are always established on the footing of their general world view or paradigm. [14] This, of course, would apply to any field of science or study and not just to biology. [15]

A paradigm is likened to a super-theory or model of reality that emanates from a dominant theoretical framework, or set of assumptions. [16] As a matter of fact, Purves and Orians further indicated that the prevailing or ruling paradigm determines which problems are interesting and which are not, and it also strongly influences the responses we make to information that seems to run counter to the predictions of our paradigm. [17] You see, it is the ruling paradigm that governs how a scientist thinks, how he forms hypotheses and theories, and even how he interprets the results of experimentation. [18] As I have already stated, scientists are not alone in this behavior; we are all controlled by a world view.

THE RULING PARADIGM

After a paradigm is accepted, for whatever justification or motivation, it is infrequently questioned. As a matter of fact, all new observations will be interpreted according to this ruling model, and those observations and conclusions that are inconsistent with it are rejected or ignored. [19] The mind-controlling strength and the influence of a ruling paradigm can best be seen in the comments of Roger Lewin, an evolutionary paleonanthropologist with the American Association for the Advancement of Science. Lewin wrote that:

> **Preconceptions are rarely acknowledged, because this, after all, would be 'unscientific'. And yet preconceptions are an individual scientist's guide to how to view the world with a degree of order that allows structured questions to be asked. The anonymous aphorism 'I wouldn't have seen it if I hadn't believed it' is a continuing truth in science.** [20]
> (emphasis added)

Furthermore, it is the conditioning power of the prevailing cultural/scientific paradigm* that controls the opinions and decisions of most American "Christians." Because it is, after all, the formative influences of the prevailing mind-set in any society that determines our values and opinions prior to our becoming believers. This is the primary purpose for this present volume. As we prepare for the twenty-first century, the American church must (if it is to maintain any appearance of Biblical Christianity), return to its foundation. Whether the American church wants to admit it or not, it has fallen asleep under the powerful control of a pagan-based cultural paradigm. Church leaders fool themselves if they for one minute think that the teachings of Christ are the regulatory principles for their church denominations, ministries, and members (more about this later).

---

*The author uses the expression cultural/scientific paradigm in a twofold way. First, as an acknowledgement that America has a fundamental premise from which culturation is propagated among her citizens. Second, that as the result of the modern scientific revolution, there is the idea that only through scientific inquiry and methodology can a proper determination be formed about the truth of "all" reality. Hence it is the common notion that any idea or belief that is fostered by our culture and passed on to its youth must have earned the highly revered honor of being "scientific."

America's Original Paradigm

The way a society looks at the world and itself is primarily determined by the controlling paradigm of their culture. It is from this vantage point that a body of knowledge is built and accepted. Accordingly, that which is identified as "good knowledge" in any age is obviously biased toward the paradigm of that age. This is why paradigm shifts in any society are extremely rare. As we shall see, the ruling paradigm in the Western world for nearly 1500 years was the Hebrew-Christian view point.

Dr. Harold Lindsell, editor emeritus of *Christianity Today* (1968-1978), and a historian, plainly asserts that the Hebrew-Christian mind-set took control of Western thought within three centuries of the great Pentecost of Acts Two and remained the governing influence of the West for more than fifteen hundred years. [21] More precisely, it was under the power of this Biblical influence that our Founding Fathers settled and established this country. In this regard, Francis Schaeffer wrote that, "The Founding Fathers of the United States (in varying degrees), understood very well the relationship between one's world view and government." [22]

Additionally, in his comments about John Witherspoon (who was a Presbyterian minister and the president of the school that later became Princeton University, and quite interestingly, the only pastor to sign the Declaration of Independence), Schaeffer remarks that:

> *He linked the Christian thinking represented by the College of New Jersey (now Princeton University), with the work he did both on the Declaration of Independence and on countless very important committees in the founding of the country. This linkage of Christian thinking*

and the concepts of government were not incidental but fundamental. [23]

Witherspoon was by no means unique in this attitude among the American Founders. Terry Eastland gives a thumbnail historical sketch in the *Commentary* magazine, which I believe shows the obvious persuasion of the Founders of America in the Hebrew-Christian world view. He writes:

As a matter of historical fact, the Founding Fathers believed that the public interest was served by the promotion of religion. The Northwest Ordinance of 1787, which set aside federal property in the territory for schools and which was passed again by Congress in 1789, is instructive. 'Religion, morality, and knowledge being necessary to good government and the happiness of mankind...[therefore]...schools and the means of learning shall forever be encouraged...' In 1811 the New York State Court upheld an indictment for blasphemous utterances against Christ, and in its ruling, given by Chief Justice Kent, the court said, 'We are Christian people, and the morality of the country is deeply engrafted upon Christianity.' Fifty years later this same court said that 'Christianity may be conceded to be the established religion...' The Pennsylvania State Court also affirmed the conviction of a man on charges of blasphemy...against the Holy Scriptures. The Court said: 'Christianity, general Christianity is, and always has been, a part of the common law of Pennsylvania...not Christianity founded on any particular religious tenets; nor Christianity with an established church and tithes and spiritual courts; but Christianity

> *with liberty of conscience to all men...' The establishment of Protestant Christianity was one not only of law but also, and far more importantly, of culture. Protestant Christianity supplied the nation with its 'system of values'—to use the modern phrase—and would do so until the 1920's when the cake of Protestant custom seemed most noticeable to begin crumbling.* [24] (emphasis added)

Thus Biblical Christianity was considered by our Founders as the skeleton for American life and government. They unanimously agreed that the Creator had given clear instructions in the Bible for the successful guidance of families, churches, and governments. They believed that to ignore or violate these plain instructions would ultimately lead to disaster and disgrace. In this regard, consider the words of Noah Webster (1758-1843), who has been called *America's Schoolmaster* (see Figure **1-b**):

> *It is extremely important to our nation, in a political as well as religious view that all possible authority and influence should be given to the scriptures, for these furnish the best principles of liberty, and the most effectual support of republican government. The principles of all genuine liberty, and wise laws and administrations are to be drawn from the Bible and sustained by its authority. The man therefore who weakens or destroys the divine authority of that book may be accessory to all the public disorders which society is doomed to suffer.* [25] (emphasis added)

Concerning this quotation, it plainly seems from our present vantage point that one could be easily provoked to believe that

Webster was a prophet, and was specifically talking about Charles Darwin.

An Incredible Paradigm Shift

The foregoing facts, candidly reveal that paradigm shifts are practically impossible, especially to the extent that a whole continent or hemisphere is philosophically affected (you must remember that the Biblical Christian dominance in the West took three centuries to become established); nevertheless, by the middle of the eighteenth century there was a clearly defined and significant movement in Western thought that has been called the Enlightenment by historians that would very quickly change the philosophical, religious, and scientific texture of all the West—a movement whose philosophical residue is with us to this very day. Dr. Harold Lindsell affirms that:

> *This movement in two centuries was to do what it took the church at Pentecost three centuries to do. It would reverse what the early church had done and bring to Europe and to the West in general [the United States is definitely included in the West] the **New Paganism**.* This new paganism has dislodged the church from its key religious and cultural position and brought about what we now call the Post-Christian Era. In doing this the Enlightenment steeped itself in the writing of the Greco-Roman world into which Christianity entered at Pentecost and **added to those writings new and compelling ideas that took root and flourished in the Western world.***

---

*Paganism-The practice of polytheism. The idea of many gods and goddesses as practiced by the ancient Greeks and Romans: with the emphasis on sensual pleasures, material goods, and irreligious attitudes...heathen.

*The Enlightenment battled with Christianity in a life and death struggle. While the victory of the Enlightenment did not erase the church from history and the West, **it did unseat the church** from its primary position in Western civilization and break its hold by installing a **New Weltanschauung*** that stood in opposition to Christianity, and in turn brought the West under the control of a **New Zeitgeist**** that was secular and anti-Christian. Whoever fails to understand what the Enlightenment did cannot understand the role of the church in modern culture. Until the fact of the demise of the church as a primary factor in Western civilization is seen, the need for another reversal will not be perceived and no orderly plan will be put into operation to effect any change.* [26] (emphasis added)

Chief among the "new ideas"*** that were universalized as a direct result of Grecian based Enlightenment thinking, and one which has wormed its way into every facet of our Western culture, is atheistic evolutionism. As a matter of fact, some historians (with whom I totally agree), date from 1859—the year Darwin published his first edition of *The Origin*—as the beginning of the

---

*Weltanschauung is a German term for world view.

**Zeitgeist is a German term for spirit which in this context refers to the general intellectual, moral, and cultural climate of an era. Can be understood to include the idea of lifestyle that is in agreement with the "spirit of the age."

***The idea of evolutionism was not at all unique to modern scientific thinking. It wasn't even unique to the philosophers of Ancient Greece. Dr. Henry Morris carefully and accurately traces its origins to Nimrod who obviously received it from Satan (see: *The Long War Against God*, authored by Dr. Henry M. Morris. For more information about this excellent work and other pertinent volumes on this subject contact: Creation Truth Foundation, Inc. P. O. Box 1435, Noble, OK 73068.)

Modern Era as well as the collapse of the Biblical Christian control over Western thought. [27]

Figure 1-b. Noah Webster, a dedicated Christian, is often called America's Schoolmaster because of the many contributions he made to early American education—all of his work was plainly based on the Bible.

Furthermore, in the above quotation, while some argue persuasively that a general long term historical overview reveals gradual spiritual progress rather than long term decline, Dr. Lindsell is totally right in his assessment of our present predicament. Christians must understand that both the present culture and the church have fallen victim to paganism. Unless we fully understand that we have cancer and that it will soon kill us except we seek immediate medical attention, we very well may continue to treat the symptoms with antiseptic creme and aspirin until we die. I am convinced that the vast majority of American churches (Evangelicals included), are so deeply controlled by **selfism** (the primary product of Enlightenment-based evolutionism), that a complete secular world view dominates much of today's religious scene. To this Fran Sciacca (pronounced shock·a), adds:

> ...I have no doubt whether conservative Christianity in the United States is healthy or ill. Evangelicalism in America has been transformed from a counterculture to merely a subculture. Evangelical Christianity is being reduced to a mirror image of the larger culture. We embrace the same values, work for the same goals, and live for the same reasons as our non-believing neighbors, all the while professing that we are citizens of the kingdom of God. [28]

To determine the extent to which evolutionism has effected your present world view, carefully compare your attitudes, goals, and values with the sacred Text. When you honestly perform this self-examination, only then will you fully comprehend the extent to which evolutionism has effected your world view. Many notable scientists and historians have already meticulously scrutinized our present society and plainly admit that Darwinian evolution has grossly affected our total way of life, especially our religious life. The following comments are the conclusions of just a few of these professionals:

> It would be amiss to overlook the great power of evolution propounded by Charles Darwin in his **Origin of the Species** and by those who have followed closely in his footsteps. This theory of how things came into being and how humanoids have developed from lower forms of primate life and ultimately from the first cell has been a part of the Enlightenment heritage that has destroyed the Judeo-Christian Weltanschauung [a Biblical Christian world view] in the West. In the scientific fraternity

today the theory of evolution has reached a status where it is proclaimed to be fact, not theory, and its proponents move heaven and earth to destroy the views of any who oppose it. [29]

The basic problem of the Christians in this country in the last eighty or so years, in regard to society and in regard to government, is that they have seen things in bits and pieces instead of totals. They have very gradually become disturbed over permissiveness, pornography, the public schools, the breakdown of the family, and finally abortion. **But they have not seen this as a totality—each thing being a part, a symptom, of a much larger problem.** *They have failed to see that all of this has come about due to a shift in world view—it is, through a fundamental change in the overall way people think and view the world and life as a whole. This shift has been away from a world view that was at least vaguely Christian in people's memory (even if they were not individually Christian) toward something completely different—***toward a world view based upon the idea that final reality is impersonal matter or energy shaped into its present form by impersonal chance*** (see Figure 1-c and 1-d).* [30] (emphasis added)

As far as Christianity was concerned, the advent of the theory of evolution and the elimination of traditional teleological thinking was catastrophic...chance and design are antithetical concepts, **and the decline in religious belief can probably be attributed** *more to the propagating and advocacy by the intellectual and scientific community of the Darwinian version of evolution than to any other single factor...It was because Darwinian theory broke man's link with God and set him a drift in a cosmos without purpose or end that its impact was so fundamental. No other intellectual revolution in modern times...so profoundly affected the way men viewed themselves and their place in the universe.* [31] (emphasis added)

It, therefore, becomes extremely clear that Darwin and his disciples wooed and converted the thinking of an entire civilization with such persuasive argumentation until Darwinian faith overthrew and has replaced Biblical faith as the basis of our cultural world view. What our Hebrew-Christian mind-set was for good, the present evolutionary mind-set is for evil. Thus the mind molding potential of a governing paradigm within any civilization is limitless, and because this is true, the present socialization process possesses a latent danger for the Christian community.

This is why Christ said that believers, while they were **in the world** were not to be **of the world** (John 17:14-16), and why Paul said, "Be not conformed to this world" (Romans 12:2). The bottomline in these Scriptural statements, as well as many more just like them, is: Christians are to constantly be discerning good from evil regarding the customs, norms and values within their society. They are to "Prove all things; hold fast to that which is good" (I Thessalonians 5:21). This is especially true for leadership, because if the watchman on the wall goes to sleep, even for just an instant, a seemingly harmless decision can be made that will eventually produce a tragedy.

Probably one of the most profound and appropriate verses of Scripture within the entirety of the Bible regarding this circumstance is found in Hebrews 12:1. The rationale for this is seen in the meaning of the phrase that is translated *which doth so easily beset us*—the entire phrase is from one Greek word *euperistatos*. "The Vulgate has *circumstance nos peccatum* (the sin standing around us). Probably this is the true idea here, the easily encompassing (or surrounding), sin." [32] Dr. Ralph Earle indicates this phrase suggests, "the sin which clings too closely to us." [33] W. E. Vine remarks that this Greek phrase "describes sin as having an advantage in favor of its prevailing." [34]

Figure **1-c**. From our first conscious moment after birth, we are now overwhelmed with evolutionism——No wonder we doubt the validity of the Bible about first origins and total reality.

Figure **1-d**. Christians must build their world view on Science According to Moses.

Now what kind of sin could cling close to us, have an advantage in its favor for longevity, and thus easily beset us? I think the answer is obvious. While it could be any number of conditions, it seems that a sin that has become popular or acceptable—one that is no longer feared or known to be sin—could easily satisfy all of these prerequisites. This reminds me of the age-old story of the frog. If you suddenly put a frog in boiling water, he will quickly hop out to save his life, but if you put him in lukewarm water and gradually heat it to the boiling point, he will sit there unaware of the gradual increasing temperature, until he is cooked to death (see Figure **1-e**). Alfred North Whitehead, mathematician and philosopher from Harvard, captured the essence of this condition and its relationship in our present society when he said that:

> *...students of the history of ideas should not look for those ideas which are under constant*

discussion in any age, but instead should look for those basic assumptions which are so fundamental to a man's way of thinking that he does not even realize he is assuming them. Evolution has now become such an unconscious assumption in our society. [35]

THE ULTIMATE OBJECTIVE OF A WORLD VIEW

Purves and Orians indicate that:

*Biology [and all other major disciplines of Western thought] began a major change in paradigm a little over a century ago with the general acceptance of Darwin's theory of evolution by natural selection. The change over has taken a long time because it required abandoning many components of a **different world view**. The pre-Darwinian world was thought to be a young one in which living organisms had been created in essentially their current forms. The Darwinian world is viewed as an ancient one...in which we would not recognize...living organisms of the future if we were transported forward in time, nor organisms of the past if we were transported back in time. Acceptance of this paradigm involves not only acceptance of the process of natural selection, it also involves accepting the view that the living world is constantly evolving, but without any future 'goals.'* [36] (emphasis added)

Purves and Orians, who are two of the leading science educators in America today, make no bones about it; they openly confess that the decision to accept Darwin's views regarding the so-called origin of species was firmly based on preference and not on any scientific finding. Further, they make it clear that evolutionism necessitated a "change over" from a former world view, which, of course, was the Hebrew-Christian, Bible-based doctrine of creationism. It is as Herbert Wendt remarked, "It was not natural scientists but philosophers who prepared the way for the idea of evolution." [37]

Figure 1-e. Like the proverbial frog, the gradual nature of the evolutionary takeover of American culture has deceived many believers.

Accordingly, evolution is really more religious at its foundation than most Western scientists would like to openly admit. Nevertheless, the non-scientist is led to believe that anything disdained by the modern scientific community must be suspect. After all, anything labeled "scientific" must be true (see Figure 1-f). Of course, as I have indicated, whether or not one's view of origins is considered scientific has everything to do with the prevailing world view. Tragically, however, a diabolic framework has provided a "scientific" fog the last several generations that has obscured the real issue of this entire religious controversy (and this is a religious debate—it basically has nothing whatsoever to do with true science). The bottomline of this entire argument is simply this—who is in charge? That is, who governs our lives, our homes, our churches, our nation and our world. Does God, the eternal Creator? He should, if indeed He is the everlasting Creator, and of course, if Biblical Theism is our world view. Or does the creature govern (Romans 1:25)? Alas! Alas! I am convinced that man has asked God to leave our present Western Civilization, which is the devastating consequences of our present world view—**humanistic evolutionism**.

The clear and obvious answer to the above question (which is, who is in charge—man or God?), is explainably the ultimate and inevitable consequence of the conditioning potency of our present materialistic* world view. Dr. Schaeffer makes an interesting comment in this regard:

> *These two world views [evolutionism v. creation] stand as total in complete antithesis to each other in content and also in their natural results...It is not that these two world*

---

*Materialism (see figure 2-e, page 60)—this word in its philosophical context attempts to confirm the atheistic theory that physical matter is the only true reality and as such is the source of all physical phenomenon. Many people, especially in this context, think that materialism means love of material things, e.g. money, houses, land, etc. It can mean this. In this context, however, it carries the connotation of "particles to people" or "molecules to man," or in other words, that matter is the mother of us all. This idea is fundamental to evolutionism. R. J. Darlington, a Harvard biologist, explains evolutionary materialism as, "...a fundamental evolutionary generalization that no external agent imposes life on matter. Matter takes the form it does because it has the inherent capacity to do so...This is one of the most remarkable and mysterious facts about our universe; that matter exists and that it has the capacity to form itself into the most complex patterns of life. By this I do not mean to suggest the existence of a vital force or entelechy [a form giving cause or a vital source of energy] or universal intelligence, but just an attribute of matter as represented by atoms and molecules we know." *Evolution for Naturalists* (New York: John Wiley, 1980), p. 233. As Carl Sagan put it: "the cosmos is all that is or ever was or ever will be." *Cosmos* (Random House: New York, 1980), p. 4.

*views are different only in how they understand the nature of reality and existence. They also inevitably produce totally different results. The operative word here is **inevitably**. It is not just that they happen to bring forth different results, but it is absolutely inevitable that they will bring forth different results.* [38] (emphasis added)

Figure 1-f. Many—even Christians—believe that scientists only speak the truth. However, scientists base many of their conclusions are based in faith just like non scientists, especially in matters of first origins.

It is just that simple! If you live with the wolves, you will learn to howl. Not only so, and far more serious, if we mingle with the heathen, we will learn their ways—we will then worship at their altars, and if we worship at their altars, we will sacrifice our children "there" (see Figure **1-g**).

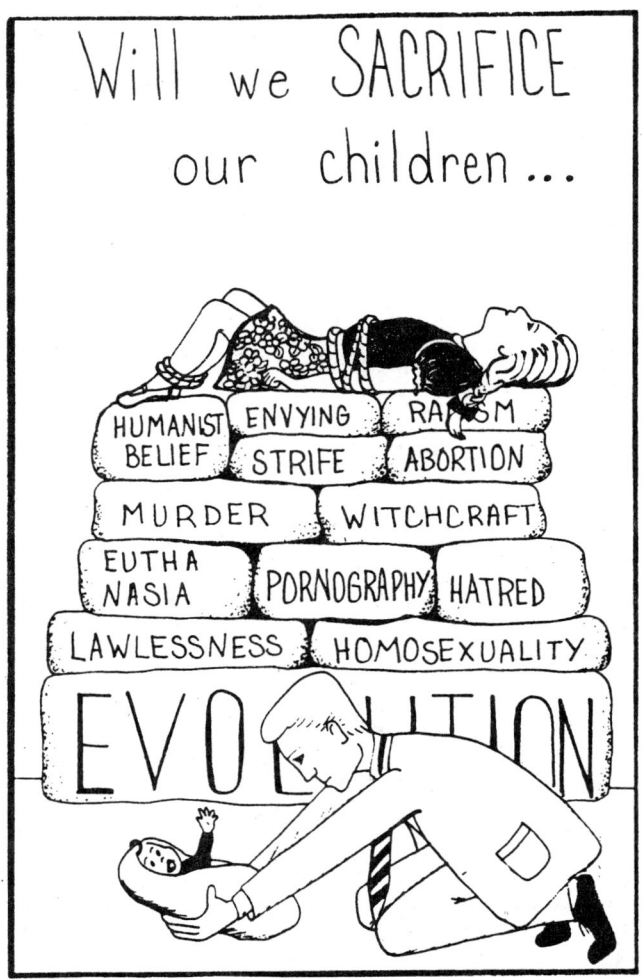

Figure **1-g**. Fathers will either train their children to love God or they will sacrifice them on the alter of humanism.

Figure **1-h**. Fathers must train their sons and daughters to see the world from God's point of view. If they don't, someone else will train them from another perspective.

Christians must base their faith, build their world view and train their sons and daughters, completely and totally on Biblical truth (see Figure **1-h**). Since the origins (foundations), of the Christian faith can be found only in the first eleven chapters of Genesis, then it stands to reason why it becomes vital for us to build our lives on that Biblical source. We must predict what we expect to observe both spiritually and physically. We must interpret what we actually see in the present, and we must explain the evidence that remains from the past from that vantage point alone. Thus we will believe unwaveringly that God is Sovereign over all, and is working all things for the blessing of the redeemed. This is Science According to Moses! This is a Biblical world view.

We must not allow the media, the educational systems of men, and the many other extensions of an evolutionary culture to enter our homes or our churches without thorough exposure, and replacement with appropriate Biblical education. To do this effectively, pastors, teachers, parents, etc., must prayerfully and diligently apply themselves to the task of unqualified repentance, fervent prayer and ardent study—the only path to a genuine revival among Christian believers. Only this kind of radical behavior and Christian reconstruction will bring a return of the historic Biblical Christian Faith of our Fathers!

Chapter 2

Mixture: The Curse Of The Fall

MIXTURE: THE CURSE OF THE FALL

──OVERVIEW──

"I am still convinced that until we are clear on what man is we shall not be clear about much else."

D. Elton Trueblood
*****

"So God created man in his own image, in the image of God he created him; male and female he created them."

Genesis 1:27, NIV
*****

"This was the foundation of the preeminence of man, of his likeness to God and his immortality: for by this he was formed into a personal being, whose immaterial part was not merely soul, but a soul breathed entirely by God..."

Keil and Delitzsch, Genesis
*****

"In any case, there can be little doubt that the 'image of God' in which man was created must entail those aspects of human nature which are not shared by animals—attributes such as moral consciousness, the ability to think abstractly, an understanding of beauty and emotion, and above all, the capacity for worshiping and loving God."

Henry M. Morris
*****

2

AT the outset of this chapter it will be necessary to make a quick comparison between man in his original created state with that of his fallen estate (Romans 5:12). This is particularly important to this chapter because it will readily reveal why it is so difficult for you and me to develop a purely Biblical world view, as well as why Paul gave such intense admonitions about world view transition to the Greek-based churches.

While it may seem that a pure and undefiled Biblical world view is illusive and unattainable in our present culture, its development is nonetheless the principal foundation from which the will of God can be truly perceived and obeyed. A Biblical world view is indeed attainable (at least in the sense that Paul spoke in Philippians 3:12-14), but only by the Grace of God and His enablement. However, its attainment must be the ultimate aim and desire for every true believer (Matthew 5:8 & 48).

Moreover, as you study the contents of this chapter, I think it is extremely important that you keep in mind the source of the original mixture which ultimately sent Adam and Eve from the presence of the Lord. Knowing that Lucifer was the source of this original deception, I hasten to add that regardless of the components or the subject matter, any ideology or philosophy that hinders or fouls the perfection of your world view and prevents you from being all that Christ intended you to be is from the same source (Ephesians 6:12). Furthermore, it is an evolutionary system that denies, resists, or compromises the absolute sovereignty of God's work of fiat creation as recorded in Genesis One. Therefore, one of the chief aims of this chapter will be to help the reader become more familiar with the anti-Scriptural nature of the many present entanglements that are directly related to our present evolutionary world view.

MAN'S ORIGINAL ESTATE

Dr. A. E. Wilder-Smith, while giving a lecture regarding the relationship between environment and heredity in human development, mentioned that man was created a hybrid of time and eternity, and that in all reality man was actually created in the "species of God." To support his view, Dr. Smith cited Genesis 1:26-27, which reads:

> *And God said, Let us make man in our image, after our likeness: and let them have dominion over the fish of the sea, and over the fowl of the air, and over the cattle, and over all the earth. So God created man in his own **image** and in the **image** of God created he him; male and female created he them.* (emphasis added, KJV)

This being true, it means that man's original being was inseparably associated with his initial Godlikeness, so that Adam was free from any **mixture** which contradicted or tainted his perception of God's will. Adam actually perceived reality perfectly. Accordingly, Adam's devotion, worship, and obedience was pure and undefiled. He could only see life from God's point of view, and therefore his "eye was single, so that his whole body was full of light." He was indeed and in truth Godlike, but when Eve disobeyed God's safeguard and partook of the forbidden tree, she, with Adam, corrupted the objective singularity of their devotion and worship. They immediately fell from the Divine ideal of knowing only "good" (cf. Matthew 19:17). Thus instantly after the fall, for the first time in their newly created lives, an insidious mixture came into their hearts, so that they could no longer just see the will of God. There was now an additional area of perceptivity within their consciousness bidding for the devotion. Herein is the diverting strength of evil, i.e. they saw both good and evil and could follow either. In other words, for the first time in their existence they became vulnerable to mixture. This danger is the apparent purpose of the Divine warning:

> *And the Lord God commanded the man, saying, of every tree of the garden thou mayest freely eat: but of the tree of the knowledge of good and evil, thou shalt not eat of it: for in **the day** that thou eatest thereof thou shalt surely **die**.* (Genesis 2:17, emphasis added)

Discernably then, the most disastrous effect of the "fall" was that man was now faced with a plethora of moral choices. He is now either cursed or blessed by his moral decisions and to complicate the process, he is now making his decision from an open forum of ideas, which obviously includes ideas alien to the will of God. This destruction of man's original and undefiled relationship with God, his Creator, from that time until now has, in effect, been an albatross around the necks of God's people and has grossly affected their world view and lifestyle ever since. Where does he go from here? The answer to this question is a matter of history! One thing is certain, his decisions have forever been tainted with the corrupting agents of philosophical mixture. Thus we see the obvious meaning of the clause, "...for in the day that thou eatest therefore thou shalt surely die" (Genesis 2:17).

The lethal nature of this condition is this: man is now open and vulnerable to attack from demonic mixture because he knows both good and evil and has a choice. Therefore, when man's environment suddenly became supercharged with enticing, desirous alternatives that appealed to a side of his nature he has heretofore not known, suddenly his decision making processes became confusing. Thus we can easily understand why the Holy Scripture is replete with warnings and instructions regarding the potential peril and devastation of being spiritually polluted because of philosophical mixture.

It is at this point that considerable obscurity prevails in the minds and hearts of many professing Christians. Many believe that conversion cures all—world view included. That is simply not the case. When you and I were converted to Christ through faith that was generated by the spoken word (Romans 10:17), we were indeed *"rescued* [translated in KJV] *from the dominion of darkness and brought to the kingdom of the Son...in whom we have redemption, the forgiveness of sins"* (Colossians 1:13-14, NIV). In other words, we were positionally moved from one kingdom to another kingdom by a sovereign act of grace through faith in the saving work of Christ. However, the "image" and "mind of Christ" is not yet realized.

Man's Greatest Task

We must remember that before we were converted we were all *"dead in trespasses and sins,"* furthermore, we habitually followed the course and fashion of this world—a world that is under demonic control (Ephesians 2:1-2, Amp. Ver.). It must be understood that initial conversion, while it transfers the repented believer from one kingdom to another, clearly does not eradicate his old world view. This deliverance can only be received through the continued work of the grace of Christ in cooperation with our deliberate, diligent, and consistent exposure to the Word of God and prayer—a daily discipline that washes our hearts and renews our thoughts! The Apostle Paul often spoke of this sanctifying process like this:

> *You were taught, with regard to your former way of life, **to put off your old self**, which is being corrupted by its deceitful desires; to be made new in the attitude of your **minds; and to put on the new self**, created to be like God in true righteousness and holiness.* (Ephesians 4:22-24, NIV; emphasis added)

> *Therefore, I urge you, brothers, in view of God's mercy, to offer your bodies as living sacrifices, holy and pleasing to God—this is your spiritual act of worship. Do not **conform*** any longer to this world, but be **transformed** by the renewing of your mind. Then you will be able to test and approve what God's will is—His good, pleasing and perfect will.* (Romans 12:1-2, NIV; emphasis added)

The dilemma of our day, one that seriously encumbers a believer's world view transformation (a process that is, and must be, subsequent to conversion), is the slippery disposition of the

---

*Dr. Ralph Earle writes: "CONFORMED—this is syschematizesthe which occurs only here and in I Peter 1:14. It comes from syn, 'with' or 'together', and *schema*, which means 'form.' So the English word conform (con, with;) exactly expresses the idea. The present Imperative means 'stop being conformed.' WORLD—the term *aion* is translated 'world' 38 times in KJV and 'age' only twice, but the later is the more usual meaning of the term. TRANSFORMED—the verb is metamorphroo. The word comes from *meta*, 'across,' and *morphe*, 'form.' It means to change across from one form to another. The biological expression 'metamorphosis' comes from it. Sanday and Headlam bring out the difference between the Greek words to 'conform' and transform' [of our verse in Romans 12:2] with this paraphrase: "Do not adopt the external and fleeting fashion of this world, but be ye transformed in your inmost nature." (Ralph Earle, *Word Meanings*, p. 199). Sounds like world view adjustment or even replacement to me!

evolutionary based culture from which we have formulated our pre-conversion world view. Because evolutionism is the fundamental orientation for American culture today, everyone of us has been terribly affected by its faith killing philosophy. As a result, the ramifications of evolutionism are plentiful and they are mind-boggling! Modern evolutionary ideas and their applications, like "strongholds," are extremely difficult to throw down (II Corinthians 10:4-5). This difficulty is reinforced by both the subtlety and abundance with which evolutionary ideas appear. For example, the disciplines of economics, political science, American history, literature, psychology, philosophy, education, theology, and science—to name just a few of the areas that have been grossly influenced by Darwinian evolutionism—all constitute the ideological arena from which converted believers have formed their values and beliefs about the world. Dr. Michael Denton, a medical doctor and research molecular biologist (who, by the way, is not a Creationist), wrote the following astounding comments:

> *The twentieth century would be incomprehensible without the Darwinian revolution. The social and political currents which have swept the world in the past eighty years would have been impossible without its intellectual sanction, [this statement was first published in 1985]. It is ironic to recall that it was the increasingly secular outlook in the nineteenth century which initially eased the way for the acceptance of evolution, while today it is perhaps the Darwinian view of nature more than any other that is responsible for the agnostic and skeptical outlook of the twentieth century. What was once a deduction from materialism has today become its foundation.*
>
> *The influence of evolutionary theory on fields far removed from biology is one of the most*

*spectacular examples in history of how a highly speculative idea for which there is no really hard scientific evidence can come to fashion the thinking of a whole society and dominate the outlook of an age. Considering its historic significance and the social and moral transformation it caused in western thought, one might have hoped that Darwinian theory was capable of a complete, comprehensive and entirely plausible explanation for all biological phenomena from the origin of life on through all its diverse manifestations up to, and including, the intellect of man. That it is neither fully plausible, nor comprehensive is deeply troubling. One might have expected that a theory of such cardinal importance, **a theory that literally changed the world**, would have been something more than metaphysics, something more than a myth.* [39] (emphasis added)

What Christians must thoroughly comprehend is that they have been socialized (conditioned), in a culture in which evolutionism is the world view. Accordingly, our "besetting sin" becomes the many behaviors and attitudes that have been produced by an evolutionary mind-set that we fail to change even though we've been converted to Christ for years. What makes this phenomenon so "besetting" is that we don't realize our thought life is so instilled with evolutionary assumptions and conclusions. Rene Dubos, one of our nations leading ecologists, made this eye-opening evaluation about evolutionism in today's world:

Most enlightened persons now accept as a fact that everything in the cosmos—from heavenly bodies to human beings—as developed and continues to develop through evolutionary processes. The great religions of the

West have come to accept a historical view of creation, [namely, the Gap Theory, Day-Age Theory, Theistic Evolution, etc.]. Evolutionary concepts are applied also to social institutions and to the arts. Indeed, most political parties, as well as schools of theology, sociology, history, or arts, teach these concepts and make them the basis of their doctrines. [40]

Figure 2-a. Herbert Spencer (1820-1903), applied Darwinian evolution to biology, psychology, sociology and many other fields.

So it is that Darwin's "idea" of struggle and survival by natural selection from simple forms to complex ones (later Darwin adapted Spencer's well known phrase "survival of the fittest"), was assimilated and carefully incorporated into all fields of thought and practice. Moreover, the application of many of Darwin's ideas have been totally swallowed by believers, and used along with Scripture for doctrine and practice.

Figure 2-b. Thomas Chalmers (1780-1847), a Scottish theologian, developed the Gap Theory (formerly called the Ruin/Reconstruction Theory—see the note at the bottom of page 277), in fear that the newly formed doctrine of uniformitarianism would discredit Genesis One. He shouldn't have...and it hasn't!

DARWINISM'S CHIEF IMPLICATION

The implications caused by this incredible infusion of anti-Scriptural ideology into our Christian culture has been earthshaking to say the least. Regretfully, there isn't space available in this volume to thoroughly treat the many vital details of this phenomenon. However, it seems that the most notorious factor produced by this takeover, and one that has reacted equally well with all of the above mentioned disciplines, is summarized by the word "progress."

The idea is that since all things are a product of evolutionary processes, then all things are quite naturally in a state of developmental progress. It is an accepted idea in Darwin's evolutionary scheme that this developmental progress is upward in nature, simple to complex. Proof for this hypothesis is, of course, nonexistent. Therefore, evolutionary scientists have no idea where or how this progression started nor where it is going. Nevertheless, progress, the by-word of our present culture, gains its status from its evolutionary connection. This idea can be illustrated by the present evolutionary explanation of history, the assumption upon which modern historians work. Today history is studied primarily from the perspective that man has evolved from a primitive, prehistorical past. As such, historical progress is explained from the standpoint of man's continual development from the slime of his remote origin to the towers of his Wall Street office. Therefore historical progress is seen only as an evolutionary process—simple to complex—with nothing but meaningless chance, unpredictable accident, and fickle randomness as the guiding mechanism. Where did we come from? They (the historians), don't have the foggiest notion! Where are we going? They don't know that either! However, they are sure, they say, that progress and change have been the guide to man's historical past.

Don't get me wrong, this is not to say that there isn't a legitimate use of the idea of progress. That is, a progress that is determined by the will of God (Joshua 1:7-8). The danger today, because of the evolutionary pressure on our thinking regarding the idea of progress is its relationship to its ideological first cousins relativism and pragmatism. Accordingly, the idea of evolutionary progress provided an apparent "scientific" foundation for the notion that all is in a state of flux. This idea has been added to the evolutionist's case against the validity of Biblical absolutism, and as a result an apparently sound "scientific" case is offered in support of moral relativism and pragmatism.

A pathetic impact of this kind of progress was felt in America when Darwinism was superimposed upon our social affairs (a sociological phenomenon called Social Darwinism). As a result, government, law, education, commerce, theology, etc., were all manipulated by this evolutionary concept of progress and soon took on patent evolutionary characteristics. A discussion of this evolutionary effect in our American society can be seen in greater detail in Chapter Four. However, with the Biblical absolutes for governing society all being discarded, evolutionary thinkers adapted forms of the so-called laws of competition, capitalism, imperialism, scientific racism, etc., all of which are familiar contents of the twentieth century, and all of which are the mere by-products of the new Darwinian society. As such, certain American entrepreneurs (e.g. Carnegie and Rockefeller); the "fittest" members of the human race (white northern Europeans); certain governmental theories (Marxism and Humanistic Capitalism); and certain educational methods (Dewey's instrumentalism and Watsonian behaviorism), were all self-proclaimed examples of evolutionary progress and survival.

A further trademark of this "progress" was relativism's kid brother—the one with a college education—Mr. Existentialism. The idea incorporated in this term was nothing new, but now it seems to be supported by science. I am sure that most of you have heard of the term *existentialism*. Sometimes it is also referred to simply as *relativism*. In case you haven't, Webster's Ninth New Collegiate Dictionary defines this term as: "a chiefly 20th century philosophical movement embracing diverse doctrines but centering on analysis of individual existence in an unfathomable universe and the plight of the individual who must assume ultimate responsibility for his acts of free will without any certain knowledge of what is right or wrong or good or bad." [41]

DARWINISTIC SCIENCE

There were many precursory developments in both European and American society that accumulated the necessary weight to tip the balance in favor of this evolutionary attitude.* However, once this idea was conceived, it gained converts rapidly, even in the Christian community, until today it is the dominant influence governing morality in America. The rationale being: if man and his society are developing by evolutionary processes, then, the orthodox Christian idea of Biblical absolutes must obviously be no longer valid. Truth, to the existentialist, is relative—it is transitional, progressive, and always changing. Evolution demanded that truth must also evolve or else it could not meet the needs of an ever evolving world. Therefore, it was concluded that man doesn't learn truth any more by revelation contained in an ancient, outdated Jewish book; he learns truth by experience; by trial and error; by social processes! In effect, he learns truth by empirical science! It was believed that the Bible had served its purpose, but now man and his society had evolved past its usefulness (see: Auguste Comte). To find truth today one must find it scientifically or else it cannot be found.

Thus it is easy to see that one of the most lethal effects of Darwinism was released into the world of ideas. What a tragic idea! Modern man now thinks that he has "scientific" license to

---

*If you are interested in further reading into the contributory developments referred to above by the terms existentialism or relativism, etc.—you should investigate August Comte and his ideas of positivism; Herbert Spencer and his evolutionary social structure; William E. Channing and Ralph Waldo Emerson and the inroads of deism, unitarianism, utilitarianism, and transcendentalism, into the mainstream of conservative Christianity. Also, Charles S. Peirce and William James and the development of the philosophy of pragmatism, all of which were strengthened by the force and popularity of evolutionism. For example, "it is written that conservative Calvinists did not abandon the field to the Unitarians in New England, but after 1805, when they 'captured' Harvard, the liberals were dominant" (Garraty, p. 247).

discard God, the Bible, and the Church—that he is free from any accountability to a Sovereign Creator. Thus "Science" has made him autonomous.* Professor John A. Garraty of Columbia University wrote that: "The effects of Darwinism on philosophy were less dramatic but in the end far more significant. Fixed systems and eternal verities were difficult to justify in a world that was constantly evolving." [42] So it was, the evolutionist said, man had come of age. He could now, because of evolutionary progress, take charge of his own world and guide his own destiny.

In this regard, I draw your attention to Sir Julian Huxley, one of the leading evolutionists of the twentieth century:

> *It is essential for UNESCO to adopt an evolutionary approach...the general philosophy of UNESCO should, it seems, be a scientific world humanism, global in extent and evolutionary in background...**Thus the struggle for existence that underlies natural selection is increasingly replaced by conscious selection, a struggle between ideas and values in consciousness.*** [43] *(This quotation is taken from the writings of Sir Julian Huxley, who was the first director-general of UNESCO —United Nations Educational Scientific and Cultural Organization—and a leading biologist*

---

*AUTONOMOUS—"Nothing in the universe is *autonomous*, save God himself. This word is an English word derived from two Greek words that are transliterated *autos* (self), and *nomos* (law). Nothing in the creation generates its own conditions of existence [or is a law unto itself]. Every fact in the universe, from beginning to end, is exhaustively interpreted by God in terms of His being, plan, and power". Gary North, The Divine Covenant (Tyler, Texas: Institute for Christian Economics, 1982), p. 2. It is therefore totally impossible for man to be autonomous in any way.

in the first half of this century). (emphasis added)

Hence the commonality within the major disciplines of modern American society is now evolutionary "progress" —progress that removed God from serious consideration; progress that set the Bible on the shelf of obsolescence by denying its Creator and His law; progress that set man on the throne over his own affairs. Is this really progress?

So now we study Sociology, which is man's relationship with other men, but without the moral imperatives of the Ten Commandments. [44] We study Psychology, which looks at man's spiritual and mental disposition, but without the knowledge that man was created in the image and likeness of God, and has fallen because of sin and needs a Savior. [45] We study Law, which is indeed nothing more or less than the will of God, but is now reduced to the egotistic wills and opinions of unconverted men (politicians, judges, lawyers, etc.). We study science, which means knowledge, but now our knowledge is void of Truth (Colossians 2:8). We study History, which is really HIS-story of man and man's dealings with his Creator, but since evolution has eliminated God from history, all that is left to study are the selfish exploits of man against man in his "struggle for life." [46] We study educational methodology, which is meant to instruct man so that he receives wisdom unto salvation, but now, without a Creator, we are teaching subjects that tell us more and more about less and less, until eventually we will receive a degree having majored in nothing (II Timothy 3:7; see Figure **2-c**). [47] We study Philosophy, which simply means the love of wisdom, but wisdom gained without the oversight of a loving Creator is a cruel joke (Colossians 2:8). [48] We study Polity, which concerns the delegated authority given for social order by a loving Creator, but without absolute authority, who has the jurisdiction to delegate (Romans 13:1)? The world of ideas and disciplines becomes a helpless tautology (that is, they are lost in a hopeless circle of human opinion).

It should be obvious to you by now that to remove God and His Word from our American culture is the same as removing the foundation from beneath a building. Without its support it collapses and falls! Jesus said it very plainly:

> *Therefore everyone who hears these words of mine,* [the Sermon on the Mount], *and puts them into practice is like a wise man who built his house upon a rock. The rain came down, the streams rose, and the winds blew and beat against that house;* **yet it did not fall, because it had its foundation on the rock.** *But everyone who hears these words of mine* **and does not put them into practice** *is like the foolish man who built his house on sand. The rain came down, the streams rose, and the winds blew and beat against that house,* **and it fell with a great crash.** (Matthew 7:24-27, NIV)

"I have studied more and more about less and less until I now know ALL there is to know about NOTHING!"

Figure 2-c. Evolutionism has so infiltrated our present educational system until the entire curriculum is based on its false assumptions. (II Timothy 3:7)

Our foundation is everything! We build upon it! We rest upon it! We trust it in times of storm! We hope for the future because of it! Of all other entities in our life, our foundation must be permanent, tried, and dependable. Is it any wonder then that America is in the plight she is in today—gang wars, rampant sexually transmitted disease, political corruption, domestic ruin, etc., etc. All because we thought we were wise; however, in our own conceit we foolishly rejected the foundational security of the "Chief Cornerstone" (Acts 4:11; Ephesians 2:20). Then we rebuilt our country, our society, and our homes on the precarious sands of evolutionism. What a calamity!

AMERICA: HER PURPOSE

Why is the Bible so vital to America? The answer to this question is readily comprehensible—the Bible is inseparably intertwined in our history and culture. America was settled by men who were Biblical Christians. Biblical Christianity was an integral part of our early governments. Any leader or office holder must first be a committed Biblical Christian before he could hold office. Our Founding Fathers established this great green place called the United States of America on the Rock of His Holy Word! This is not to say that there weren't opportunists and evildoers also woven into the fabric of our beginnings. History is, of course, replete with their pernicious deeds (many there were in this group who even professed Christianity). Be that as it may, anyone who takes a pensive look at our country's origins must admit that America was all about freedom—especially religious freedom! I should add, a particular kind of religious freedom. The renowned Patrick Henry said it best:

> *It cannot be emphasized too strongly or too often that this great nation was founded, not by religionists, but by Christians; not on religion, but on the Gospel of Jesus Christ!*

> *For this very reason peoples of other faiths have been afforded asylum, prosperity, and freedom here.* [49]

Why is this statement not found in today's history textbooks? Did Patrick Henry make this evaluation from supportable facts? Was he just a hot-headed extremist? A mere provincial bigot? Or was his assessment a valid narrative about our nation's founding? I'll let you be the judge.

Just before going ashore after their long voyage from England aboard the Mayflower (November, 1620), the Pilgrims committed to parchment and endorsed the noteworthy Mayflower Compact. It clearly declares their purpose and commitment:

> *...having undertaken for the Glory of God, and advancement of the Christian faith...a voyage to plant the first colony in the northern parts of Virginia...[we] combine ourselves into a civil body politic for...[the] furtherance of the ends aforesaid.* [50]

Moreover, in 1629 the Charter of Massachusetts posits:

> *...our said people...may be so religiously, peaceably, and civilly governed, as their good life and orderly conversation may win and incite the natives of [that] country to the knowledge and obedience of the only true God and Saviour of mankind, and the Christian faith, which is our royal intention, and...the principal end of this plantation...* [51]

About ten years later, the Puritans, under the leadership of John Winthrop also came to America. In his book, A Model of Christian Charity, Winthrop identified the importance of their witness to their purpose for coming to this wilderness land. He said that:

> *This love among Christians is a real thing, not imaginary...We are a company, professing ourselves knit together by this bond of love...Thus stands the cause between God and us: we are entered into covenant with Him for this work. We have taken out a Commission; the Lord hath given us leave to draw our own articles...to do justly, to love mercy, to walk humbly with our God; For this end, we must be knit together in this work as one man...* [52]

> *For we must consider that we shall be as a city upon a hill, the eyes of all people are upon us, so that if we shall deal falsely with God in this work we have undertaken, and so cause Him to withdraw His present help from us, we shall be made a story and by-word through the world.* [53]

Winthrop's words exude with commitment and purpose and are piercingly recriminating to the present-day purpose of the modern Church. However, this does not end the record!

The Maryland Charter (1632) presented Lord Baltimore's goals for the Maryland colony as follows:

> *Our well beloved and right trusty subject Caecilius Calver, Baron of Baltimore...being animated with a laudable and pious zeal for extending the Christian religion...hath humbly besought leave of us that he may transport...a numerous colony of the English nation to a*

> certain region...partly occupied by savages having no knowledge of the Divine Being. [54]

Upon reaching the land that became Maryland, it is recorded that they:

> ...took possession of the country 'for [the] Lord Jesus Christ' and made "Christianity the established faith of the land... [55]

A little more than ten years later (1647), William Bradford wrote in the first American History called *Of Plymouth Plantation* that:

> ...a great hope and inward zeal they had of laying some good foundation...for the propagating and advancing the gospel of the kingdom of Christ...their desires were set on the ways of God, and to enjoy His ordinances...they rested on His providence and knew whom they had believed. [56]

Moreover, the Charter granted to the Quakers and Christian groups for the establishment of the colony in North Carolina stated their intent to be "...the propagation of the gospel...in the parts of America not yet cultivated and planted.." [57] Furthermore, the Charter granted to Roger Williams for the colony to be called Rhode Island (1663), set forth terms in keeping with the attitude of the other colonies:

> The colonies are to pursue with peace and loyal minds their sober, serious, and religious intentions...in holy Christian faith...A most flourishing civil state may stand and best be maintained...rightly grounded upon Gospel principles. [58]

In 1731, the southeastern area known today as the state of Georgia was settled by several minority Christian groups, including the Moravians. It is written that after they "touched shore," they:

> ...kneeled in thanks to God...[and said], 'Our end for leaving our native land is not to gain riches and honor, but singly this: to live wholly to the glory of God.' Their object... was 'to make Georgia a religious colony' ...they invited John and Charles Wesley and Rev. George Whitefield over to serve as chaplains, oversee Indian affairs and build orphanages, etc. When Whitefield died, the legislature attempted to have him buried there at public cost in honor of his influence. [59]

Additionally, David Barton remarked that *"the charter of Connecticut, New Hampshire, and New Jersey were virtually a restatement of the Christian goals reflected in the other charters".* [60] The more we truly learn about American history, the more it becomes obvious that the history of America, to a great extent, is nothing more than the history of the rise and fall of Biblical Christianity. Quite simply, it is plain to see that our Founders possessed a strong conservative Biblical faith. Therefore, we can easily identify the permeation of Biblical values throughout early American life and society. Due to this Biblical leadership, we observe the sacred intent of our early colleges and universities. Furthermore, it was this sacred Biblical orientation that caused the United States of America to become the greatest Christian missionary enterprise of all times. As the result of the Bible's decline, we witness the subjugation of the Christian community by paganism. Eventually, we see the tragic fall of

Biblical Christianity as the major influence in American culture. American history, therefore, is actually the record of the ascension and decline of the Bible in our culture, with its decline being directly related to the rise of evolutionary materialism.

However, our original faith in, and obedient respect for, the Bible, is without question! As the result, God has truly shed His grace on America. It is beyond debate, the many physical, technological, and spiritual advantages that America has enjoyed for so many years are not due to some inherent goodness or personal merit of our ancestors. It was due, however, to the fact that the grace of God led our Forefathers to love God and His word. This is a vital idea and one for which there are tons of documentation. It was their love for the Creator that caused our Founders to love His church and His message—for which they sacrificed, and why so many of them died—to establish these same godly principles in the foundation of this country.

In this regard, therefore, the words of our Founding Fathers are extremely important. In a circular letter to the governors at the close of the War of Independence (1783), General George Washington wrote (see Figure **2-d**):

> *I now make it my earnest prayer that God would have you, and the State over which you preside, in His holy protection...that He would most graciously be pleased to dispose us all to do justice, to love mercy, and to demean ourselves with that charity, humility, and pacific temper of mind, which were the characteristics of the Divine Author of our blessed religion, and without an humble*

imitation of whose example in these things, we can never hope to be a happy nation. [61]

Moreover, in this same attitude of the heart and keeping with the resolution of Edmund Randolph, on July 4, 1787, the entire Constitutional Convention met together at the Reformed Calvinistic Church and were addressed by minister William Rogers. Consider carefully the content of Rev. Roger's prayer offered at the opening of this meeting:

...we fervently recommend to thy fatherly notice...our federal convention...Favor them, from day to day, with thy inspiring presence; be their wisdom and strength; enable them to devise such measures as may prove happy instruments in healing all divisions and prove the good of the great whole...that the United States of America may form one example of a free and virtuous government...May we ...continue, under the influence of republican virtue, to partake of all the blessings of cultivated and Christian society. [62]

Finally, to further show the consensus of Bible influence in our founding, I refer to a statement made by John Jay.* Jay was one of the three authors of The Federalist Papers, Washington's choice for the first Chief Justice of the United States Supreme Court, and a member of both the First and Second Continental

---

*I highly recommend to you David Barton's brilliant work *The Myth of Separation*. In Barton's work you will find ample validation of our Christian heritage. To obtain Barton's work or other appropriate materials—Contact: Creation Truth Foundation, P. O. Box 1435, Noble, OK 73068.

Congresses (during which he served one time as its President). Jay said that:

> *Providence has given to our people the choice of their rulers, and it is the duty as well as the privilege and interest of our Christian nation to select and prefer Christians for their ruler's.* [63]

Much additional data could be amassed in support of our early Biblical faith, but that will have to wait for another study.* The main point, however, and the primary reason for which I have now injected this idea, is that as long as Biblical Christianity remained in custody of the values and laws of American society, her general world view also remained, for the most part, consistent with Biblical absolutes. This provided a basic Biblical continuity between the greater society and the community of believers. By this, I am not disparaging the need for saving grace—God forbid—but I am saying that if the greater culture is essentially Christian, as it was in our earlier history, then the above stated purpose for which God used America is easier facilitated; also kindred to this purpose is the training of Christian converts and Christian children.

EVOLUTIONARY MIXTURE IN EVANGELICALISM

Even though I will show in Chapter Three the incredible depth in which evolutionism has burrowed into the thinking of modern believers, for convicting emphasis, I feel at this time, I

---

*It is interesting, as well as revealing, [to see] Jay's deep commitment to Christianity [and] to note that he also served as president of the American Bible Society for many years. On his deathbed, when asked if he had any final words for his children, he replied, "They have the Book". John Jay, The Correspondence and Public Papers of John Jay, 1794-1826, Henry P. Johnston, ed. (New York: Burt Franklin, 1970), Vol. IV, p. 154. Also cited in Barton p. 119.

must show how evolution has affected Evangelical thought and life. A key to understanding the nature of this influence is seen in the Apostle Paul's warning that during the "last days" believers could easily become victimized by a perilous self-love (II Timothy 3). The major theme today that is echoed from the media, commerce, industry, religion, etc., is abridged in the phrase *"Be all you can be..."* Fran Sciacca said that:

> *The early seventies saw the release of numerous books focusing on self, such as Robert Ringer's 'Winning Through Intimidation,' and 'Looking Out For Number One,' Wayne Dyer's 'Your Erroneous Zones,' and 'Pulling Your Own String,' and Sherwin Cotler's 'Assertion Training,' to mention a few. The seventies saw the birth of Self magazine and paved the way for the current obsession with popular psychology.* [64]

One does not have to be a serious student of history to take notice of the fact that every time man is freed from the restraints of his personal accountability to an Absolute Authority, his behavior becomes increasingly *self*-motivated, until hedonism* becomes the rule of the day. This can be historically observed in one form or another in the downfall of Israel, Babylon, Greece, Rome, Egypt, England and America—among others.

Hedonistic attitudes are now so deeply instilled in America's world view that *"**feelings** (the barometer of pleasure), and **self** (the recipient of pleasure), are the two most pampered and pandered items on nearly every agenda, from advertising to business and from education to*

---

*HEDONISM-The doctrine that advocates pleasure or happiness as the sole or chief good in life. In I Timothy 5:6 the Apostle Paul states: "Whereas she who lives in pleasure and self-gratification—giving herself [himself] up to luxury and self-indulgence—is dead even while she [still] lives" (Amp. Ver.). This verse ostensibly refers to hedonism.

religion." ⁶⁵ We are constantly bombarded with slogans that tell us—*this is your kind of place, nothing so sensual was ever so innocent*, or as the lyrics of a recent number one song boasted: *"How could it be wrong when it feels so right." "From [nearly] every billboard, TV ad, and direct-mail package comes the message that the product in question will either make you feel better, provide some sexual gratification, or improve your [self-] image."* ⁶⁶ All of these present manifestations of selfism are the direct result of a doctrine that gave scientific eminence to autonomy—the idea of self-rule.

Figure 2-d. George Washington, our first President, believed in and prayed to a personal God almost everyday of his adult life (LaHaye, p. 103).

To emphasize the perilous ground upon which we presently stand, I refer to an earlier connection made between Matthew 7:24-26 and the attitude of our Founding Fathers. That is to say, since it is obvious that our Founders did follow God's Word and did build America on a Biblical foundation, for us to now totally abandon the Rock, or what's even worse to remove that Rock as our foundation, is asking for a total collapse of our culture! Furthermore, I might add, a total collapse of our culture will be inevitable unless the holy purpose for which this nation was founded is restored. Professor James Davison Hunter in the conclusion of his report on the Evangelical Academy Project (see Chapter Five, p. 376), made this extraordinary appraisal of why his survey turned out as it did:

> ...the story of conservative Protestantism in America is in some ways the story of the pilgrim in John Bunyan's epic allegory [Pilgrim's Progress]. In his journey from the city of Destruction to the Celestial City, Bunyan's pilgrim stumbles into innumerable difficulties and temptations—from the Slough of Despond to Doubting Castle; from the Town of Vanity to the Valley of Humiliation; from Hill Difficulty to the Valley of the Shadow of Death. This is not to mention his encounters with such unsavory figures as Mr. Worldly Wiseman, Mistrust...and the like. Yet what our pilgrim (Evangelicalism) endures and Bunyan's does not is a long and sustained season in the Labyrinths of Modernity. Not only does he emerge a little dizzy and confused, but out of the experience our traveler is **transformed.** The pilgrim becomes a tourist. Though still headed toward Celestial Country, he is now traveling with less conviction, less confidence about his path, **and is perhaps more vulnerable to the worldly distractions encountered by Bunyan's pilgrim.**
> [67] (emphasis added)

Hunter's work openly displays many serious defects that can be plainly documented in the attitude and behavior patterns of present-day conservative Evangelicals. As you will see in Chapter

Five, Hunter's book is a must for anyone desirous to understand the present plight of the American church. Hunter shows that a little more than half of all Evangelicals surveyed in his study said that the "Bible is the inspired Word of God." [68] You would expect for Evangelicals to at least say this! You would also expect the percentage to be much higher. Why wasn't the percentage higher? Hunter indicates that over fifty percent of those Evangelicals surveyed said that in matters of science and history the Bible cannot be taken literally. [69] Consequently, the respondents to Hunter's survey are admitting that they believe that Darwin, and other evolutionary scientists, know more than God about the events of Creation, the Flood, the formation of the Nations, etc. That's why the percentage is not higher!

Just as Dr. Tim LaHaye advanced the idea that the Declaration of Independence is our Nation's Charter, the Constitution acts as our by-laws. Accordingly, the Constitution must be interpreted by the light of the Charter in order for it to remain in agreement with the Charter. [70] So it is with the Bible—the first eleven chapters of Genesis compose our Biblical Christian Charter, while the balance of the Bible make up our By-laws. The fact remains, to reject the Charter for any reason is to destroy the potency of the By-laws. Consequently, when one rejects the clear, literal statements of Genesis One, he opens the door for all manner of concession and appeasement, here and elsewhere in the Bible. Hunter said it like this:

> *The sentiment of the coming generation [of Evangelicals], then, is mixed. It is clear that they know they "should" believe but with that they struggle. Intellectually grasping the soteriological [pertaining to salvation] demands of orthodox Christianity is one matter; emotionally accepting them is quite another.* [71]

The reason for this struggle is easy to understand—everything in the Bible is now subjected to human rationalization because its

Charter (Genesis 1-11), has been "scientifically" discredited. Sadly, after we allow the greater culture to negatively influence our faith in the Creator and his Creative work, that same mixture will ultimately affect our own lifestyle as well. This it has done!

SELFISM: THE PERIL OF MODERN EVOLUTIONISM

Professor Hunter indicated that the greater American culture prior to the mid-1960's held to a general attitude that one's **self** (i.e. the source of pride, lust, and covetousness, etc.), was a negative phenomenon. [72] However, during the mid-sixties there was a turnabout in attitude regarding the intrinsic value of one's self. This change in feeling is seen as an "accentuation of subjectivity and the virtual veneration of the self, exhibited in deliberate efforts to achieve self-understanding, self-improvement, and self-fulfillment." [73]

Have you noticed the many significant changes in the general attitude of America towards God and His Word that found their national debut in the early and mid-1960's? While it is true, evolutionary humanism was showing up in our culture earlier in this century, it was in the early sixties that the American culture voiced approval of evolutionism as a total world view. For during this decade evolutionary efforts culminated and were blatantly articulated in all areas of our society. This is not coincidental (see Chapter Four)! Nevertheless, even though the greater culture shifted toward an excessive accent on self-appreciation, self-worth, and self-expression (which had become the ultimate aim in the reach for the good life), one would tend to think that mainstream conservative Evangelicalism would show, by comparison, considerable restraint in this area. Surprisingly, however, "there are, in fact, strong indications that a total reversal has taken place in the Evangelical conception of the nature and value of the self." [74] Hunter's findings revealed that the next generation of Evangelicals (that is, those who will be assuming leadership roles at the beginning of the twenty-first century), are as interested in themselves, their personal goals and ambitions, as are their worldly neighbors—maybe more so! What's even further staggering is that among the respondents to Hunter's three year survey, there were more non-believers than believers who perceived the Christian's role in society to be primarily for the benefit of others. Sciacca remarked, in this regard, that:

> *If the watching world honestly expects to see conservative Christians oriented outwardly, only to discover that they are as inwardly focused as the larger culture, the truth of the gospel is reduced to merely an apparent difference in lifestyle preference rather than an issue of one's eternal destiny. Faith is then understood merely as a matter of personal choice, rather than as alignment with eternal truth.* [75]

Here's the tragedy in all of this. In Luke 6:40 we read, "A student is not above his teacher, but everyone who is fully trained will be like his teacher" (NIV). To this James Baldwin adds the shocking truth that: "children have never been very good at listening to their elders, but they have never failed to imitate them." [76] Thus it seems, beyond question—the next generation of Evangelicals are already "fully trained" and will advance the ball down field for selfism farther than ever in recent history. We will have larger and more ornately designed church buildings, a better "standard" of living, more charismatic hoopla, enthusiasm, and emotionalism; but I ask—are these the characteristics of a genuine Biblical world view?

It doesn't take a Ph.D. to understand that primitive, Biblical, first century Christianity—the same Christlike attitude that motivated the likes of a Mother Theresa, or a Haralan Popoff, or a Francis Asbury, etc., etc., has somewhere been lost in the "stuff." I am not saying that Christianity demands that one take a vow of poverty in order to be committed, but I am saying—and that quite loudly—that a great majority of professing believers are far more interested in vacations, homes, clothes, buildings, recreation, automobiles, occupations, etc., than they are the personal discipline necessary to put Beattitudinal living into practice in their daily lives. I am further convinced that our present delusion is the direct result of the secularizing effects of a materialistic evolutionary mixture that came of age in our society in the early 1960's (see Figure **2-e**). It directly threw God out of the American culture in 1962-1963, and from that time it has seriously retarded the formation process of a Biblical world view in the heart of professing believers. Charles Colson corroborates the reality of the decaying influence of the culture on our present American church by saying:

> *Separated from God, men seek satisfaction in their senses. This is mindless hedonism; it is a world view in which, according to Professor Allen Bloom, 'the self has become the modern substitute for the soul'.*
>
> *A 1985 study titled* Habits of the Heart *calls this attitude 'utilitarian individualism', arguing that the two primary ways Americans attempt to order their lives are through 'the dream of personal success' and 'vivid personal feelings'. This was reinforced as those interviewed consistently defined their ultimate goals in terms of self-fulfillment or self-realization. Marriage was seen as an opportunity for personal development, work as a method of personal advancement,* **and church as a means of personal fulfillment.**
>
> *What this study reflects is simply the inevitable consequences of four decades of the steady erosion of* **absolute values.** *As a result*

> *we live with a massive case of schizophrenia.* **Outwardly we are a religious people, but inwardly our religious beliefs make no difference in how we live.** *We are obsessed with self; we live, raise families, govern, die as though God does not exist, just as Nietzsche predicted a century ago.* [77] (emphasis added)

I am well aware that for many the last eight or so pages of this chapter may be hard to believe, but as difficult and impossible as it may sound—it is nevertheless the truth! The documentation is replete. This is, sad to say, the present plight of American Evangelicalism—all due to the mixing of evolutionary humanism with the Bible. I want to close this section by discussing three aspects of this plight.

SELF HELP: DOES IT REALLY HELP?

All one has to do to justify the reality of the present self-help emphasis is to visit the local Bible bookstore. There you will be overwhelmed by dozens and dozens of titles that promise the reader personal improvement in all sorts of areas. Fran Sciacca made these eye-opening remarks:

> *And how about the world of Christian books? The most recent edition of Current Christian Books lists nearly five hundred books whose titles begins with* **How to**...*Suddenly, it's 'Biblical' to improve your sex life, lose weight, balance your checkbook, coordinate your colors, eat oat bran, break codependency, heal your past, and release your hidden personality. I am waiting on a book about, 'How to Lead Your Pet to Christ'!* [78] (emphasis added)

If this was not so serious, it would be hilariously funny. To this, Professor Hunter adds the fact that 12 percent of all the titles published among Evangelicals today deal with the importance of our need to understand or solve the many emotional or psychological complexities of being human. [79] This, of course, again shows the importance we are now placing on our "self."

Figure 2-e. Evolutionary materialism.

Just standing around the average Evangelical church today (before or after church service), is quite revealing. In casual conversation you hear terms like self-actualization, dysfunctional, and codependent—to name a few. These are terms that until just a few years ago had not yet been invented. They are the products of men like Abraham Maslow, Sigmund Freud, B. F. Skinner, etc., or one of their disciples—all of whom were evolutionary and materialistic. Thus it seems, rather than following the admonition of Christ (Matthew 7:24), or the Apostle Paul (Romans 12:1-2), we are more disposed to follow the words of those who profess to have "scientific" sanction. These wrong choices and the explanation for choosing them is clearly seen in Paul's experience in Acts 27:9-41. The point is: He told the ship's owner and the ship's captain that the voyage would sustain hurt and great damage (Acts 27:10). "Nevertheless, the centurion believed the master and the owner of the ship, more than those things which were spoken by Paul" (Acts 27:11). In other words, they believed the "expert" rather than the man of God, and total wipe-out was the result. Sciacca makes this startling comment:

> *Make no mistake, a growing number of conservative Christians in America will..read James Dobson and Larry Crabb before they'll read their Bible, even though neither of these men would ever wish this to be the case."* [80] *(Please note that Sciacca has worked with Dr. James Dobson, therefore, his remark is simply given to emphasize the present discredited status of the Bible, and its use for decision making as perceived by many Evangelicals).*

Hence, it is apparent that we have become so intoxicated with ourselves that we have either forgotten or abandoned the ultimate path to true "blessedness"—it is only found in the words of the Bible, and not elsewhere. The famous American poet Robert Frost wrote an extremely appropriate poem *The Road Not Taken*, that articulates this condition in a remarkable fashion:

> *Two roads diverged in a yellow wood,*
> *And sorry I could not travel both*
> *And be one traveler, long I stood*
> *And look down one as far as I could*
> *To where it bent in the undergrowth;*
>
> *Then took the other, as just as fair,*
> *And having perhaps the better claim,*
> *Because it was grassy and wanted wear;*

Though as for that, the passing there
Had worn them really about the same,

And both that morning equally lay
In leaves no step had trodden black.
Oh, I kept the first for another day!
Yet knowing how way leads on to way,
I doubted if I should ever come back.

I shall be telling this with a sign
Somewhere ages and ages hence:
Two roads diverged in a wood, and I—
I took the one less traveled by,
And that has made all the difference. [81]
(emphasis added)

Jesus, as well as Paul the Apostle, tells of the "path that makes all the difference" when they said:

Therefore I tell you, do not worry about your life, what you will eat or drink; or about your body, what you will wear. Is not life more important than food, and the body more important than clothes? Look at the birds of the air; they do not sow or reap or store away in barns, and yet your heavenly Father feeds them. Are you not much more valuable than they? Who of you by worrying can add a single hour to his life? And why do you worry about clothes? See how the lilies of the field grow. They do not labor or spin. Yet I tell you that not even Solomon in all his splendor was dressed like one of these. If that is how God clothes the grass of the field, which is here today and tomorrow is thrown into the fire, will he not much more clothe you, O you of little faith? So do not worry, saying, 'What

> *shall we eat?' or 'What shall we drink?' or 'What shall we wear?' For the **pagans** run after these things, and your heavenly Father knows you need them. **BUT SEEK FIRST HIS KINGDOM AND HIS RIGHTEOUSNESS AND ALL THESE THINGS WILL BE GIVEN YOU AS WELL.*** (Matthew 6:25-33, NIV—emphasis added)

> *For this reason I kneel before the Father, from whom his whole family in heaven and on earth derives its name. I pray that out of his glorious riches he may strengthen you with power though his Spirit in your **inner being**, so that Christ may dwell in your hearts through faith. And I pray that you, being rooted and established in love, may have power, together with all saints, to grasp how wide and long and high and deep is the love of Christ, and to know this love that surpasses knowledge —**that you may be filled to the measure of all the fullness of God.*** (Ephesians 3:14-19, NIV—emphasis added)

The choice is yours! You cannot walk on two paths at once. You will either follow the path prepared by the Creator, or a path of your own making (Proverbs 14:12). To genuinely help yourself, you must deny yourself and let God be your only expression.

COUNSELING MANIA

As the reality of personal sin (including pride and disobedience), became more and more minimized as the real cause for one's anxiety and guilt during the recent "selfism" revival, the propensity to seek help from the psychologist or the counselor became a growing phenomenon among Evangelicals. Professor

James Davison Hunter shares this revealing bit of history concerning Evangelicalism's mushrooming gravitation toward professional counselling:

> *[The self-help emphasis] is further supported by an expansive service industry of 'helping' professionals. Since it was founded in 1953, the (Evangelical's), National Association of Christians in Social Work has grown steadily to over 1500. Likewise, the Christian Association of Psychological Studies (CAPS; a largely Evangelical organization for clinical, pastoral, and counseling psychologists), has, since 1952, grown to a total membership of 2,350 (85% of that growth has taken place since the early 1970's). These 'experts' have specialized and are credentialed in matters of the **self**. More importantly, they derive their livelihoods from (and thus have a vested interest in), refining and perpetuating this orientation as a legitimate area of spiritual concern.* ***In doing this, these experts have freely adopted the languages of humanistic, behavioristic, and psychoanalytic psychologies*** *(all of these perspectives, for example, are widely represented among the membership of CAPS).* ***Indeed, one of the most interesting aspects of this phenomenon is the way traditional theologies are integrated with these highly secular (at least at the assumptive level), models of the person and the human psyche.*** [82] (emphasis added)

In the first place, let me quickly say that I am not trying to throw the baby out with the bathwater. I am convinced that genuine Biblical counseling is a valid ministry. However, it must be Biblical! I know counseling is emphasized throughout the

Evangelical community as a viable ministry of the church. However, it can only be viable so long as it inculcates the leadership of the heavenly Counsellor (Isaiah 9:6). If at any point along the way, the counsellor refers to or borrows the theories of modern psychology, he runs the risk of evolutionary mixture and wrong emphasis (the worst of which claims that man can help himself, solve his own problems, and forgive his own sins). No where is this emphasis seen more clearly than in the Humanist Manifesto II (the bible for the American Humanist Association):

> *...we can discover no divine purpose or providence for the human species. While there is much that we do not know, humans are responsible for what we are or will become.* ***No deity can save us; we must save ourselves.*** [83]

It is a matter of common knowledge that the popular advocates of the humanistic, behavioristic, and psychoanalytic schools of psychology were all non-believing, materialistic evolutionists of the highest magnitude, e.g. Abraham Maslow (1908-1970), B. F. Skinner (1904-), and Sigmund Freud (1856-1939), respectively. As a matter of fact, B. F. Skinner, who was a behavioral psychologist from Harvard, also was a signer of the Humanist Manifesto II. In their textbook, *Introduction To Psychology*, Hilgard and Atkinson openly reveal the evolutionary nature of modern psychology:

> *Man is a flesh-and-blood organism related to other organisms through an evolutionary history. Man's habits, thoughts, and aspirations are centered in his brain and nervous system, and whenever we study him, we study something he does or expresses through his bodily processes. We may examine a man as a vertebrate, a mammal, and a primate—as*

> *one who shares an evolutionary background with the rest of the biological world.* [84]

This is why Hunter was so surprised to find these typically "secular" schools of psychology being so smugly "integrated" into the counseling practices of professing Evangelicalism. Dr. Henry Morris (see Figure 2-g), gives additional background evidence that should automatically make the utilization of these psychological systems totally taboo for any professing Christian:

> *There is probably no academic field of study and application more thoroughly saturated with evolutionary thinking than psychology and the other fields dealing with human behavior. Ever since Darwin—and especially since Freud—psychologists, have assumed that man is merely an evolved animal and have evaluated his behavioral problems on an animalistic basis...* ***This approach is wrong because man is not an "animal."*** *He did not evolve from other life forms but was created in the image of God. Ironically, 'psychology' means the 'study of the soul', but modern psychologists do not even believe in the soul...It has always been known that Freud was an ardent follower of Darwin, but this has been even more emphasized by the recent discovery of certain papers left by him.* [85]
> (emphasis added)

Concerning these papers that have recently been found from Freud's past, Daniel Goleman writes:

> *In a 1915 paper, Freud demonstrates his preoccupation with evolution. Immersed in the theories of Darwin and Lamarck, who believed acquired traits could be inherited,*

Freud concluded that mental disorders were the vestiges of behavior that had been appropriate in earlier stages of evolution. [86]

Figure 2-f. Jean Baptiste Lamarck (1744-1829), an excellent zoologist, developed a theory of organic evolution that greatly influenced Darwin.

Dr. Morris continues:

> *In fact, most modern psychologists have now disavowed Freud even though they have built on his foundation. They, of course, still operate completely within an evolutionary framework, regarding man as merely an evolved animal, with animal problems and animal solutions.* [87]

While, as I have already stated, genuine Christian counseling can in some instances be used quite profitably, it is however no replacement for the Word of God, prayer, and the work of the Holy Spirit. As a matter of fact, counseling, to be of any benefit, must always be in strict concord with holy Scriptures. [88] Moreover, counseling alone cannot absolve the effects of sin, especially unforgiveness, pride, and doubt. The only successful antidote for these maladies of the human heart is the atoning, cross-work of the incarnate God—the Lord Jesus Christ! I am reminded of a line in that great hymn written by Robert Lowery: **What Can Wash Away My Sins, Nothing But the Blood of Jesus**! I am deeply saddened that selfism, the uppermost fruit of evolutionism, has so mixed with our modern theological understanding, that many trusting and desperate souls have yielded their lives, and the lives of their families, to the barrenness of a counseling chamber or the desolate island of a psychiatrist's couch. It seems, the loving care of the heavenly Comforter and the steady guidance of the eternal LOGOS are no longer desirable or considered a useful intervention for a troubled heart in our complicated society. How sad! What is even more distressing and eye-opening, is that one of America's leading Evangelical seminaries in 1990 awarded more than 40% of her degrees in counseling "rather than in theology, missions, or Christian education." [89] This relocation of emphasis among those considered Biblically conservative is a solemn, decisive portent that marks the depth of our departure from the clear teaching of the Bible. You see, this shift in emphasis from theology (the study of God and His attributes), to psychology (the study of the psyche or self), openly violates the teaching of the Word of God. Moreover, the two exclusive points of concentration in modern psychology are the **past** and the **self**—both of which according to the New Testament are to be forgotten, crucified, and avoided—NOT "remembered," "fulfilled," and "esteemed" (Philippians 3:13, Galatians 5:24, II Timothy 3:5).

The words of Dr. J. I. Packer cannot be overlooked nor improved upon in this context. In a unique way, he pinpoints the subtle way evolutionary humanism has surfaced in Evangelicalism, and in so doing underscores what I have been saying. In his Introductory Essay to the reprint (1959), of John Owen's *The Death of Death in the Death of Christ* (1647), Packer said:

> *There is no doubt that Evangelicalism today is in a state of perplexity and unsettlement. In such matters as the practice of evangelism, the teaching of holiness, the building up of local church life, the pastor's dealing with souls and the exercise of discipline, there is evidence of widespread dissatisfaction with things as they are and of equally widespread uncertainty as to the road ahead. This is a complex phenomenon, to which many factors have contributed; but, if we go to the root of the matter, we shall find that these perplexities are all ultimately due to our having lost our grip on the **Biblical Gospel**. Without realizing it, we have during the past century bartered the gospel for a substitute product which, though it looked similar enough in points of detail, is as a whole a decidedly different thing. Hence our troubles; for the substitute product does not answer the end for which the authentic gospel has in past*

*days proved itself so mighty. The **new gospel** conspicuously fails to produce deep reverence, deep repentance, deep humility, a spirit of worship, a concern for the church. Why?* **We would suggest that the reason lies in its own character and content. It fails to make men God-centered and God-fearing in their hearts because this is not primarily what it is trying to do.** *One way of stating the difference between it and the **old gospel** is to say that it is too exclusively concerned to be "helpful" to man—to bring peace, comfort, happiness, and satisfaction—and too little concerned to glorify God.* *The **old gospel** was "helpful," too —more so, indeed, than is the **new**—but (so to speak), incidentally, for its first concern was always to give glory to God.* **It was always and essentially a proclamation of Divine sovereignty in mercy and judgment, a summons to bow down and worship the mighty Lord on whom man depends for all good, both in nature and grace.** *Its center of reference was unambiguously God.* **But in the new gospel the center of reference is man.** *This is just to say that the **old gospel** was religious in a way that the **new gospel** is not.* **Whereas the chief aim of the OLD was to teach men to worship God, the concern of the NEW seems limited to making them feel better. The subject of the OLD GOSPEL was God and His ways with men; the subject of the NEW is man and the help God gives him.** *There is a world of difference. The whole perspective and emphasis of gospel preaching has changed.* [90] (emphasis added)

Figure 2-g. Dr. Henry M. Morris, the father of the present scientific and Biblical creationist revival, is the Founder and President Emeritus of the Institute for Creation Research (El Cajon, CA).

Having carefully read this incredible quotation—all that I can say—indeed, all I need to say is that, it is a matter of record that evolutionary humanism has definitely left its brand on American Christianity. This is no where more evident than in our present-day infatuation with counseling. God help us!

BEATITUDINAL VS. ATTITUDINAL HOLINESS

This is the last of the three aspects in this series, but please be aware that many additional and important departures in faith have been caused by the evolutionary takeover of our culture. These three (self-help emphasis, godless counseling, and attitudinal holiness), however, are the most obvious and the most dangerous. It is truly my prayer that you are now beginning to see what I mean when I refer to evolutionary mixture. For it is indeed subtle, and it has definitely been designed to block the fulfillment of your Christian maturity. This last point is probably the most lethal one of all.

To begin with, then, I must assert that the Biblical standard demanding Christian holiness and heart purity is absolute and is not left to our disposition or choice. Jesus said, "Be ye therefore perfect even as your Father which is in heaven is perfect (Matthew 5:48, KJV). He would not have said this if it were not attainable, and furthermore since an absolute perfection, in the same sense that the Father is perfect, would be unattainable by sinful man, it seems the perfection to which Christ referred was comparative (i.e. to the same degree the Father is perfect in His absolute Holiness, we are to be perfect in Kingdom character). Accordingly, it goes without saying that the Beatitudes of Matthew 5:3-11 are Christ's definitive presentation of the characteristics of the

Kingdom of God. Therefore, as D. Martin-Lloyd Jones so ably said:

> *There are certain general lessons, I suggest, to be drawn from the Beatitudes. First,* **all Christians are to be like this.** *Read the Beatitudes, and there you have a description of what every Christian is meant to be. It is not merely the description of some exceptional Christians. Our Lord does not say here that He is going to paint a picture of what certain outstanding characters are going to be and can be in this world. It is His description of every single Christian.* [91] (emphasis made by author)

Thus we see holiness as Beatitudinal, and not attitudinal! It is based on Christ's desires and demands—not ours!

In light of this, however, let me ask you a serious question. Do you know any congregation that would rather be faithful to a ten-part series of two hour Bible studies, which give thorough exposition to the Beatitudes, more than they would like to participate in church-league basketball, celebration-night singspiration, or any number of other church social events I could mention? No, and neither do I! That's the problem! So, what has the modern Evangelical church done? It has curtailed the Bible studies and built family life centers. After all, success is measured by numbers and the majority are simply not interested in being "pure in heart!" We would rather be slim and trim and athletic. This is not to say that bodily exercise is not profitable, for it is; there is nothing wrong with bodily exercise in the right time. Yet, any profit gained from bodily exercise is vastly overshadowed by the profit one can gain from Bible study. Paul put it this way:

> *...exercise yourself rather to godliness. For bodily exercise profits a little, but Godliness is profitable for all things, having promise of the life that now is and of that which is to come* (I Timothy 4:7-8, NKJV).

The point is not whether bodily exercise is profitable, rather it is, sad to say, that an overwhelming majority of Evangelical Christians would rather participate in a church related activity, under the guise of religion, than they would truly "seek first the Kingdom of God and His righteousness" (Matthew 6:33). This simply means that we are more in love with ourselves than with God (II Timothy 3:1-5). What compounds this problem is that the church has also given vent to many other wayward propensities in our culture!

It seems churches feel that only those with the best programs will have the crowd, and since crowds mean money, the modern church seeks the most appealing program instead of the power of God. This effect is selfism gone to seed, and the ultimate design in evolutionism (II Thessalonians 2:4). This is what Fran Sciacca calls "recreational holiness," and what Dr. Gordan McGee calls "Hollywood Holiness." Does it work? You be the judge.

The recent resurrection of "selfism" is not without its own unique harvest. We are witnessing unprecedented, even epidemic level, adultery and divorce within Evangelical churches. The extent of this moral collapse is even found among national church leaders, televangelists, local pastors, and the believers next door, and in the next room. [92] Furthermore, we are seeing the break-up of the Christian home in landslide proportions. This condition is reflected in the attitude of the greater culture. George Gallup, Jr. and Jim Castelli reported that:

> *There has been a dramatic change in attitudes toward premarital sex in the past generation. In 1969, 68 percent of Americans said it was wrong and only 21 percent said it was not. By 1985, for the first time, more Americans said that premarital sex was not wrong (52 percent) than that it was (39 percent)...**The 1988 survey found that 43 percent of churched Americans said premarital sex was always wrong and...13 percent said it was almost always wrong; 23 percent said it was sometimes wrong and 15 percent said it was not wrong at all.*** [93]

This plainly means that 51% of the churched respondents to this survey believe that premarital sex is permissible. If you sow to the wind, you will of the wind reap a whirlwind (Hosea 8:7). The greatest of all divine laws is the Harvest Law—you will indeed reap what you sow (Galatians 6:7). Who do we think we are? Do we really believe we can sow self-expression and self-actualization and reap Biblical holiness? Regrettably, we really do believe this, and the evidence verifies that we do—we are far more intoxicated with self than ever before. As a community, American Christians have never before been as morally destitute as we are today.

It is for this same selfish reason that a "growing number of Christians demand that their church service be exciting, fresh, stimulating, and relevant—the basic ingredients of the entertainment industry. We have become a generation of pewsitters waiting for the show to begin. When the show at one church no longer maintains our interest, we simply find a better one elsewhere." [94] Thus because of these nomadic church members, we find new churches being either started or built in large numbers all over America. It is also quite common to hear someone remark when asked if they attend church: "No, not regularly," they will answer, "but we are still visiting around!" Regardless as to whether or not the Bible approves of our attitudinal behavior is of little consequence any more, because we are discernably not interested in the clear facts of Holy Scripture. We continue to tramp around from place to place attempting to find the church of our choice—and what is that church like? It must entertain us above all else. We want to laugh, cry, sing, dance, be emotionally lifted to the stars. We like style and glamour—but despise structure and content. Don't you dare say that divorce is sin, adultery is immorality, AIDS is a moral issue, abortion is murder, homosexuality is a travesty, and that my ease-loving noncommittal attitude is a slap in the Creator's face. This will immediately send us packing—On The Road Again—looking for the church of our choice because that kind of convicting, exposing, Bible preaching is certainly not our choice. If we look long enough and hard enough we will find a church that fits our "self"; but, "Does it conform to the standard of God?", and more importantly, "Is it the local body into which the Holy Spirit has placed you?" These should be the questions with which we are concerned.

Even more tragic and destructive to the Kingdom of God is the build-a-new-church syndrome. For some, if they don't find their "kind" of church, they simply start one (which only compounds selfism). What does this sad, but true, scenario reveal? It reveals that the Bible doctrines of commitment, spiritual covering, submission, chain of command, and the doctrine of the local church with our placement in it by a sovereign act of the Holy Spirit (I Corinthians 12:18), are all foreign to a growing majority in today's Evangelical camp.

The truth of the matter is that "selfism" has so supercharged our cultural thinking that we are following after its allurements as did the mice after the Pied Piper in Browning's poem. While we may deny this allegation, our behavior betrays us. Autonomy has become our secret purpose—but, oh dear reader, autonomy is the "essence of sin" (Isaiah 4:13-15).

Additionally, autonomous behavior is an attitudinal response that is derived from a free-wheeling culture that is convinced that God and His Word provide a scientifically untenable explanation for first origins and total reality. It is the flagrant usurpation of the total authority and the Holy prerogatives that alone belongs to God, the Eternal Creator! "It is an invasion of God's right to rule His own creation. It is making one's own self to be his own god. It is putting too much emphasis on what self wants, with too little concern about what God wants." [95] It is a broad way that leadeth to destruction! To this Fran Sciacca adds:

> But under inspection, it becomes clear that we [the Evangelical church in America] are as self-indulged as the larger culture, and nearly as autonomous. This secularization is a serious deviation from God's plans for His people, and as such constitutes large-scale spiritual decay. **This places the next generation at risk more than all the ills of society combined. And the reason they are at risk is a consequence of the age-old way that world views are passed from one generation to another.** [96] (emphasis added)

The battle lines are clearly drawn. Accordingly, in the twilight of this twentieth century, there is an overwhelming and desperate need for men and women to love God and His Word more than anything else, and to become abandoned to the cause of spiritual and academic training both for themselves and their sons and daughters. They must dedicate themselves to a modern Spiritual Awakening: a Reformation of Biblical truth; a Renaissance of faith in the absolutes of God's Word; a Recoronation of God to the throne of affairs in His visible Church; and a Reconstruction of the Holy foundation for all God's work among men (Genesis 1:1).

The only way this can ever happen is for God's people to return to the Bible with all of their heart! This does not mean another religious meeting, or another conference, or another workshop, or another retreat—for the most part these have all become arenas of "selfism"—but, family by family, man by man, we must return to daily, diligent, disciplined Bible Study, fervent prayer, and love for God. The first and most vital phase in this awakening requires the complete and unqualified return to our Christian foundation—IN THE BEGINNING GOD CREATED...! Only this kind of intense and thorough revival can save us. Only in the heat of a Holy conflagration of this magnitude can human selfism be totally melted away in your life and mine—from the church! Then, and only then, will we once again have the cultural setting necessary for the propagation of our Biblical Christian world view. This will not happen without a fight! We must engage the enemy? I pray we do.

CHAPTER 3

WHAT IS REAL KNOWLEDGE?

WHAT IS REAL KNOWLEDGE?

— OVERVIEW —

The reverent and worshipful fear of the Lord is the beginning and the principal and choice part of knowledge—that is, its starting point and its essence; but fools despise skillful and godly wisdom, instruction, and discipline.

Proverbs 1:7, Amplified Version

* * * * * *

Scientific knowledge, while it is entirely suitable for working with physical matter and living organisms, is radically unsuitable for the study of first origins and total reality. After all, how does one scientifically experiment with beginnings, especially since man came along at some point after the beginning?

G. Thomas Sharp

* * * * * *

All men by nature desire to know.

Aristotle

* * * * * *

Always learning and never able to come to the knowledge of the truth.

3

It is important to keep in mind, as you read this chapter, that scientific investigation and the subsequent development of knowledge about the physical world—its many processes and its many cause/effect relationships—is a legitimate pursuit and is mandated by God. [97] There is nothing wrong with good science (and there is good science), but science is limited to the here and now. In other words, there is a clear and well understood demarcation that exists regarding the usefulness of scientific inquiry with regard to the development of modern technology, industrial practices, medicine, etc., and the so-called scientific commentary about first origins and total reality.* Without a doubt, dependable knowledge has been developed from the incorporation of scientific procedure. This has led to many useful

---

*Dr. John Moore gives the following valuable information in this matter: "...*it is important for scientists and non-specialists in the twentieth century—the Scientific Age—to comprehend that areas of inquiry are different. When scientists use such words as "could," "seem," or "perhaps," in their assertions about first origins, which of necessity must be of the past, they are not truly hypothesizing. It is so very important...to show the difference between ideas scientists have about naturally occurring events in the present and ideas scientists have about supposed events in the past. Yet someone may urge that speculative statements and extrapolations are components of scientific work. This is true when speculations and extrapolations are confined within dimensions of size and time wherein tests and possible corrections of ideas can be attempted and accomplished in the lifetime of a given set of investigators. But speculations about first origins are forever beyond any possible test or correction by empirical, quantitative, mechanical studies involving careful, orderly scientific work.* John Moore, *How To Teach Origins* (Milford, Michigan: Mott Media, Inc., Publishers, 1983), p. 83.

technological advancements and improvements. However, any attempt to use science, even legitimate science, as a means of explaining first origins or total reality is simply asking science to do something it is not capable of doing.

Nevertheless, this is exactly what has been done, and is still being done! Supported by so-called "scientific" knowledge, we are told today that God does not exist, supernatural creation is out of the question, and the Bible has no bearing whatsoever on what constitutes real knowledge about first origins and total reality. However, the Apostle Paul indicated to the contrary. He said that anyone who looks honestly at the physical world—"the things that are made"—are simply "without excuse,"—if they do not plainly recognize the signature of the Creator in all that they observe (Romans 1:20).

HOW DOES MAN CHOOSE KNOWLEDGE

Technically, there's not a hair's breadth of difference between the definition of science and knowledge. After all, science means knowledge! Moreover, it is an extremely long and complicated story to trace how science (as we understand it), came to be used as the benchmark for assessing the disparity between reliable and unreliable knowledge (see Figure **3-a**). I will attempt to tell as much of the story as is comfortably possible in a single volume. I pray that you will be inspired to read and study further after you have read these pages.

Let it suffice, for the time being, to say that for almost fifteen hundred years, Western man used the Bible as his chief source of knowledge, especially about first origins and total reality (see Figure **3-b**). That is to say, the earth was considered to be young; all species fixed within the narrow corridor of each "created kind;" the earth's topography explained by catastrophism

Figure 3-a. All true education leads to a greater knowledge of Jesus Christ, the eternal Creator. Tragically, modern academia has lost this pursuit for real knowledge (c.f. II Timothy 3:7, 14-16).

(especially Noah's Flood), etc. It has only been since the late 1200's that movements of anti-Biblical thought were introduced with enough impetus to sustain growth so that the Bible eventually became discredited in the minds of many people. Furthermore, this process did not take place overnight—it wasn't until the beginning of the nineteenth century that the headquarters of darkness had accumulated enough strength to seriously challenge the Hebrew-Christian world view in the West. Yet they did and evolutionism has taken its place! Today, atheistic evolutionism has become the world view in America and Western Europe, and therefore the anchorage for our knowledge base (this is especially true in the centers of education, media, law, religion, science, etc.). The degree to which the foregoing is true can be seen in the remarks of Alfred North Whitehead (1861-1947), Professor of Mathematics and Philosophy at Harvard:

> *...students of the history of ideas should not look for those ideas which are under constant discussion in any age, but instead should look for those basic assumptions which are so fundamental to a man's way of thinking that he does not even realize he is assuming them.* ***Evolution has by now become such an unconscious assumption in our society.*** [98] (emphasis added)

Even though evolution, in the name of "good" science, has become the "unconscious assumption in our society," still, in such matters as the origin of the universe, the origin of life, the origin of species, etc., scientific probing and investigation cannot answer the questions of "how" and "when". For that matter, in 1983 Gordon R. Taylor wrote in the book *The Great Evolution Mystery* that of all the mysteries of biology, the most baffling is the question of how life arose on earth. [99] As a matter of fact, life itself, not withstanding its origin, is a mystery to scientific understanding for the very reason that all living organisms are made up totally from nonliving elements. What causes them to live? As we shall see, the illusive answer to this question as with all questions about first origins and total reality have occupied the debate of philosophers, theologians, and scientists for time immemorial.

While it is not the purpose of this chapter to examine these several opinions, it must be clearly understood by the reader that only two basic models* exist from which an opinion about first origins and total reality can be drawn. You will either build your world view from the demands of a Biblically literal creationist, or you will build your world view from the demands of a naturalistic evolutionary model—there are no others. The evolutionist, Douglas Futuyma, who received his Ph.D. from the University of Michigan and is the author of a widely used textbook on evolution called *Evolutionary Biology*, wrote:

> *Creation and evolution, between them, exhaust the possible explanations for the origin of living things. Organisms either appeared on the earth fully developed or they did not. If they did not, they must have developed from preexisting species by some process of modification. If they did appear in a fully developed state, they must have indeed have been created by some omnipotent intelligence, for no natural process could possibly form inanimate molecules into an elephant or a redwood tree in one step...* [100]

---

*The model to which you subscribe will be determined by your belief system. By this I mean your propensity to accept the explanations of materialistic, nonbelieving scientists, or your reliance on the Bible as the source for true knowledge about first origins and total reality is determined by the model you have chosen, for whatever reason, to accept and follow.

Thus your viewpoint about ultimate reality will either be based on the model of supernatural creation with all of its ramifications (what I have chosen to call *Science According To Moses*), or else it will be developed from an evolutionary perspective (that is, science according to man's reason). Furthermore, it is a matter of record, for the most part, that the model of choice in any given historical period is determined by the prevailing world view at that time. [101] The prevailing world view, therefore, is of utmost importance, because it is from this view point that all facts are, at any given time, considered and interpreted.

Figure **3-b**. Revelation is the vocabulary of human reason ...Without revelation, reason is meaningless. (Psalm 119:130)

THE INSEPARABLE RELATIONSHIP OF KNOWLEDGE AND WORLD VIEW

As we stated in chapter one, for 1500 years or so (that is, from approximately 325 A.D. until about 1850 A.D.), the Hebrew-Christian mind-set was generally the accepted viewpoint in Western culture. For example, it was customary that men believed God to be the Creator, that life came from Him, and that species were fixed within created "kinds." Thus the evolutionary idea later proposed, which stated that the development of a new species over long periods of time and through the work of fine gradations from existing species, was not a part of accepted knowledge during this time period. In other words, the world view of Western thought during this time period was Biblical Theism.*

At the outset, it must be understood that acceptable knowledge about total reality at any time or place is completely dependent upon the philosophical system that is embraced at the time. In this regard, the big question that I want to discuss in this chapter is as follows: Knowing that our world view determines our knowledge base, and that our knowledge base controls our understanding of first origins and total reality—can we really scientifically discern with our five senses or from inductive logic alone the great questions of life, such as—*Who am I?...From whence did I come?...Where am I going?...and Who is really in charge?* Or is it really faith and revelation that are the instructors of the human heart for truth in these matters? Even though generation after generation of greater thinkers than I have considered these questions, they must be dealt with and answered in our generation also.

Can these questions be answered? Yes, I believe they can, for even in the face of these timeless enigmas, the Lord Jesus did not hesitate to say, *"If you continue in **my word**, you are truly my disciples, and you will **know the truth**, and the truth will make you free"* (John 8:31-33). Some may argue that the words of Jesus are no different than those of any other

---

*BIBLICAL THEISM—This expression is understood to refer to God as defined and verbalized in Scripture. Namely that, He is sovereign, eternal, immutable, omnipotent, omnipresent, and omniscient. Furthermore, this view is monotheistic as seen in Deuteronomy 6:4, and espouses the literal accounting of Genesis One as the only reliable explanation for first origins and total reality.

religious teacher or philosopher. They argue that His words are just as exclusive and biased as others. This would be a valid comment if Jesus was but a mere man. However, if Jesus is the eternal God incarnate, then His words take on a completely different nature and value, especially for Christian disciples. Where the Christian believer is concerned, to whom the text of this book is specifically addressed, the words of Christ are final and absolute and all debate is hushed before His holy counsel.

It is, however, a historical fact that Christianity was deliberately and thoroughly mixed with pagan thought during pre-Renaissance times. This mixing of ideologies ultimately opened the door to doubt and misgivings about the authenticity of the Bible among Christian leaders. In turn, it eventually gave rise to the atheistic materialism that developed during the "Age of Reason". Evolutionism, the logical conclusion of the "Age of Reason" with all of its faith killing commentary, would not have had a chance to persuade or influence one member of the Lord's church, if the Christian church would have "earnestly contended" for a knowledge base about all reality that is strictly Biblical and Christian. Alas, this was not the case.

As modern science, during the late 1700's, took a left turn in its philosophical point of view and began traveling the road of materialism, many influential church leaders motivated by the fear and uncertainty that modern science would disprove the book of Genesis made all manner of concessions and comprises (e.g. The Ruin-Reconstruction Theory, Progressive Creationism, Theistic Evolution, and the Day-Age Theory—to name a few). All of this was nothing more than mere attempts at harmonizing the Genesis account of Creation with the new "scientific" findings. However, Genesis does not need any scientific findings for its support! It is the Word of God—isn't it? Furthermore, as we have now totally discovered, the supposed scientific basis for evolution was not scientific at all!

The beauty and unique difference between Biblical Christianity and all other philosophies of the world resides in transcendental nature of Jesus Christ. He was both God and man—the God-man. The fact that the eternal Creator became man to redeem His fallen creation is without equal in all other religions of the world. More incomparable than that is the fact that Jesus perfectly relegated His redemptive actions to the frailty of a human tabernacle (that is, He effected redemption, defeated the devil, and lived an exemplary life in the confines of a totally human tabernacle—John 5:19). Since the bottomline in Christian discipleship is to follow Christ's footsteps, this forever settles for all disciples of Christ, from whence their knowledge source is to be derived (John 17:17). This means that for the Christian community faith and revelation based on Biblical knowledge must be our source for understanding first origins and total reality. Any mixture will weaken the truth and will ultimately produce a pseudo-Christian system.

What good is a pseudo-Christian church, or a church that is half Christian and half pagan: or for that matter, what good is a so-called Christian church with any paganism mixed with its doctrines and practices at all? It seems to me that Jesus gave an appropriate answer to these questions when He plainly stated:

> *He that is not with me is against me; and he that gathereth not with me scattereth abroad.* [10]

This probably sounds trite, but by definition, to be Christian is to be Christlike. If that is true, then bias, or no bias, the Christian church should at all costs maintain its distinctive Christlike world view and lifestyle. Dr. Francis Schaeffer addressed the contradiction that is apparent in today's church community by comparing the profession with the possession of modern "Christians." He said that:

> *These two world views [creation v. evolution], stand as totals in complete antithesis to each*

> *other in content and also in their natural results...It is not that these two world views are different only in how they understand the nature of reality and existence. They also inevitably produce totally different results. The operative word here is **inevitably**. It is not just that they happen to bring forth different results, but it is **absolutely inevitable** that they will bring forth different results.* [103] (emphasis added)

The true nature of these "inevitable consequences" was presented in clear and graphic detail by Dr. Richard Hofstadter when he said:

> *Whenever the Darwin-Malthus system is applied, its consequences are bad: in sociology a hard-hearted indifference to the sufferings of the poor; in religion, atheism; in philosophy the dark wastes of German pessimism, and a contempt for the value of human life which, like Stoicism in Rome, presages social catastrophe.* [104]

In other words, whether it is "scientific or not scientific," university approved or not university approved, the foundational source of knowledge concerning total reality, for the Christian disciple at least, is "the fear of the Lord!" (Proverbs 1:7). Many modern Christians simply do not understand this. They have accommodated modern science by changing clear Scriptural positions about Creation, the Flood of Noah, the formation of the nations, etc., in an attempt to harmonize the Bible with modern "science." In so doing, they have corrupted the clear Biblical distinctive that is necessary for perpetuating the Christian world view. The Christian believer should rather let the Bible speak for itself, and then explain the world and all that is in it in the light of Its teachings. [105] Dr. Schaeffer indicated that many reasons have caused Christians to deviate from a distinct Biblical stance, but he says the primary cause is a defective view of Christianity itself. [106] Schaeffer contends quite forcefully that *"Christianity is not just a series of truths but **Truth**—truth about all reality"* [107] *(emphasis Schaeffer's).* Biblical Christianity is not just a religious system organized by men; it is a revelation of the will of the eternal Creator delivered to us by His only begotten Son. I must quote on this subject the incomparable words of Arno Clemens Gaebelein, D.D. Their equal, I believe, cannot be found written among the thoughts of man:

> *Is then our Christianity such an attempt to solve the problems of human existence, a searching for the truth, or a philosophical effort to explain God, the universe, man, his origin and relation to the supreme Being? If so, then it is a religion and must be classed with the other existing religious systems, which have been in the past and which are in the world today. If such is the case then Christianity is as unable to give assurance to man, or to satisfy the soul-hunger of man, or to bring man back to God, as the other religions are unable to accomplish this result. If so, then Christianity is not trustworthy. Furthermore, we should be forced to look for something else, something which man needs and which is not found in Christianity.*
>
> *It would then be entirely logical, to say, as is being said today among the ever increasing rationalists in Christendom, that since Christianity is a religion, it has defects as other religions have defects, that it is, for this reason, not the final religion. Modernism is aiming at this very thing. This movement tries to strip Christianity of certain elements, thus*

> *reducing it to a religion, and, having accomplished this, to produce a new religion, better suited to the needs of the times than Christianity. This is the goal of Modernism. Is Christianity a religion? NO!* **Christianity is supernatural revelation.**
>
> *We have learned that in the Old Testament is found the supernatural revelation of God. Christianity is the highest of all supernatural revelation. What is supernaturally revealed in Christianity is final; there can be no higher revelation than that which is given in Christianity. If Christianity is robbed of its supernatural character then it is mere religion and has no more power to save man, to bring the knowledge of God to the starving souls of men, than Buddhism, Brahmanism or Confucianism. This robbery of the supernatural element of Christianity is being carried on today.* [108] (emphasis added)

It is because Christianity—in its purest form—is indeed a revelation of the Creator to His children and was furthermore effectuated by the Creator himself that Schaeffer, Gaebelein, and others can make such exclusive statements. Jesus was not just another man, He was the eternal Creator "in whom dwelleth all the treasures of **wisdom and knowledge** (Colossians 2:3). Hence for the Christian to seek knowledge about first origins and total reality from any other source, other than the Bible (as a primary reference), is not only futile, it is blasphemous! This is not to say that the Biblical model of origins does not have overwhelming evidence in the natural world—it does! For the believer, however, the Bible must be our standard and final authority on all matters (cp. John 3:12).

The Founders Of Modern Science Were Creationists

Real knowledge (scientia), about all reality was perceived as being revelational in nature during the period in which modern science arose (about 1500-1850). It was commonly believed among the early scientists that, *"All scripture is God-breathed* and is profitable for doctrine, reproof, correction, and instruction..."* (II Timothy 3:16). Dr. Henry Morris, who is the founder and president of the largest creation science research institute in the world (Institute for Creation Research in El Cajon, CA), made the following assessment of this situation (see Appendix C):

> *...most of the great scientists of the past who founded and developed the key disciplines of science were creationists.* Note the following sampling:
>
> *Physics (Newton, Faraday, Maxwell, Kelvin)*
> *Chemistry (Boyle, Dalton, Pascal, Ramsay)*
> *Biology (Ray, Linnaeus, Mendel, Pasteur)*
> *Geology (Steno, Woodward, Brewster, Agassiz)*
> *Astronomy (Kepler, Galileo, Herschel, Maunder)*
>
> *These men, as well as scores of others who could be mentioned, were all creationists not*

---

*The phrase *"Given by inspiration"* (KJV) is translated from one word—*theopheistos*—and literally means *"God-breathed"* (NIV). Dr. Earle indicates that *"God breathed His truth into the hearts and minds of the writer of Scripture"* (Word Meanings, p. 409). Josephus employed a very similar term concerning the O.T. books. He said the writers wrote according to the *pneustia* (the inspiration) of God. The Jewish philosopher Philo, who was contemporary with Josephus, referred to the Holy Scripture as *"theochrest oracles;"* that is to say, oracles given under the agency and dictation of God. L. Gaussen, The Divine Inspiration of the Bible (Kregel Publications: Grand Rapids, Michigan, 1971), pp. 23-24. Gaussen also indicated that "Theopneustia is not a system, it is a fact; and this fact, like everything else that has taken place in the history of redemption, is one of the doctrines of our faith" (p. 24).

> evolutionists, and their names are practically synonymous with the rise of modern science. To them, the scientific enterprise was a high calling, one dedicated to "thinking God's thoughts after Him," as it were, certainly not something dedicated to destroying creationism. [109] (emphasis added)

Not only did these truly great scientists believe that the Biblical account of creation was the proper explanation for first origins, it is also extremely well documented (as Dr. Morris alluded), that due to their faith and confidence in the orderly workings of the Creator God, they were inspired to conduct the scientific investigations which gave rise to the modern scientific era. Dr. John Moore, who was professor of Natural Science at Michigan State University prior to retirement, wrote the following eye-opening comments regarding how these great scientists were strongly affected by their belief in Biblical Creationism:

> These early scientists, [men like Tycho Brahe, John Ray, Johannes Kepler, Isaac Newton, Robert Boyle, and many others], believed that the universe, including the earth, was created by a reasonable God. Insisting upon the rationality of God as intelligible, early scientists believed that they could look for the explanation of any event in terms of earlier events, that is, cause and effect. They also believed that God created an orderly universe with uniformity of natural events...The universe was not random...and the universe was "open" because God had intervened in the activities of human beings.
>
> Further aspects drawn from the Christian world view by early scientists were: (1) belief in the certainty that objective reality existed

—there was something "there" that could be studied successfully; and also (2) belief that the natural environment was worth studying— for to do so was to investigate God's creation.

This was possible further, because they believed that human beings were created in the image of God, that human beings could find out about natural things because they had been given dominion as God's creation over all things. [110]

Thus modern science was begun by those who believed the Bible to be the guide for their predictions and investigations concerning man, the heavens, and the earth. Dr. Moore continues:

*In particular, these first modern scientists believed that God as the Creator established lawful relationships in His creation which could be discovered. Not only was God the giver of laws of human conduct, but He was the Lawgiver of the laws of nature as well. The idea of laws in the universe and special methods of inquiry that could be used to discover such laws (**God's laws, not Nature's laws**), was another important part of the Christian base that made modern science possible. To a great extent **all** scientists, since the time of the early greats...to the present naturalistically oriented, non-believing scientists, must rely on the principles first drawn from this Christian base...* [111] (emphasis added)

It seems only logically sound to me that if the likes of an Isaac Newton, or a Louis Pasteur, or a Gregor Mendel, etc., could not see a need for separation between the Biblical account of creation and true science, then neither should anyone else. Alas, a change was in the air (even while these great men were alive).

The Knowledge Base Shift Was Not Scientific

The shift in thinking from the Biblical Christian foundation to today's pagan orientation (which ultimately led to our present materialistic, nonbelieving, evolutionary knowledge base), was gradual and slow, but was extremely strategic and persistent in nature. This transition can be easily traced in history, and many fine accounts have been written on the subject. It becomes evident to anyone who takes the time to look that the conflict between these two knowledge bases (or world views), is deeper and more involved than just the superficial movements of history. For example, it is now completely mind-boggling to both the creationist and the evolutionist alike that Darwin's famous book *The Origin Of Species*, being so utterly void of any real scientific findings or evidence, could have so thoroughly transformed the thinking of Western Europe and America. Dr. Morris writes about this anomaly as follows:

> *...one can search the whole book [The Origin] in vain for any real scientific evidences of evolution—evidences that have been empirically verified and have stood the test of time. No proof is given anywhere—no examples are cited of new species known to have been produced by natural selection, no transitional forms are shown, no evolutionary mechanisms are documented. Actually, the whole book is most notable for its complete lack of documentation. It is all speculation, special plead-*

ing and ad hoc assumptions. None of The Origin's *evidences or arguments have stood up under modern critical analysis, even by other evolutionists. One can only marvel that such a book could have had so profound an influence on the subsequent history of human life and thought.* **There is bound to be something more here than meets the eye!** [112] (emphasis added)

To give additional significance to the mystery surrounding this astonishing scientific fiasco, it is now a matter of record that Darwin, in his two principal works (*The Origin of Species* and the *Descent of Man*), introduced his arguments over eight hundred times with the expression, "we may well suppose (see Figure **3-e, p. 106**)." [113] This is not exactly sound scientific procedure as most anyone should realize. How then could anything so devoid of reality become so colossally accepted? It is in all respects nothing more than the age-old collision between the kingdom of God and the kingdom of Satan. With this idea in mind, let's begin a historical investigation for the roots of modern evolutionism.

I have chosen to begin the accounting of this conflict between the two kingdoms with an investigation of the philosophical climate in Western Europe at the time of the Renaissance. The humanism that arose out of the Renaissance (1300-1650), together with the rationalism, skepticism, and raw materialism that congealed during the Enlightenment (1700), provided the philosophical setting for the shift in world view that can be distinctly seen in Western thought during the late 1800's. This change, from Biblical revelation to that of scientific materialism regarding first origins and ultimate reality, was therefore produced by philosophy and not real science. You see, modern evolutionism was conceived in an unbelieving climate. Accordingly, any attempt to justify the validity of evolutionism on the basis of scientific findings is simply an exercise in futility. The evidence for this statement is overwhelming. Consider the testimony from the following professional witnesses:

> **WITNESS NO. 1** Wolfgang Smith, who received his doctorate from Massachusetts Institute of Technology and is Professor of Mathematics and Physics at Oregon State University, wrote:
>
> *And the salient fact is this: If by evolution we mean macroevolution* then it can be said with the utmost rigor that the doctrine is totally bereft of scientific sanction...there exists to this day not a shred of bonafide scientific evidence in support of the thesis that macroevolutionary transformation has ever occurred [Figure 3-c].* [114]

> **WITNESS NO. 2** L. Harrison Matthews, a professional zoologist and a fellow in the Royal Society of London (the oldest and most renowned scientific organization in Great Britain). He also wrote the introduction to the 1971 edition of Darwin's *Origin of Species* that was published by J. M. Dent & Sons LTD. In this Introduction he quite remarkably confesses that:
>
> *In accepting evolution as a fact, how many biologists pause to reflect that science is built upon theories that have been proved by experiment to be correct,* **or remember that the theory of animal evolution has never been thus proved?***...proof has never been produced,*

---

*MACROEVOLUTION simply refers to the total evolutionary process, as that explained by Darwin, that can ultimately result in a large scale change of considerable complexity (as in species to species formation).

*though a few not entirely convincing examples are claimed to have been found. The fact of evolution is the backbone of biology, and biology is thus in the peculiar position of being a science founded on an **unproved theory**—is it then a science or a faith? Belief in the theory of evolution is thus exactly parallel to belief in special creation—both are concepts which believers know to be true but neither, up to the present, has been capable of proof.*
[115] (emphasis added)

Figure **3-c.**

WITNESS NO. 3 Dr. Errol I. White, a professional paleoichthyologist (one who studies fossil fish), and who during his 1966 presidential address to the

Linnaean Society (a highly prestigious scientific organization in Great Britain), said:

> *And this brings me to the real point of the address—what I might describe as an imaginary dilemma of my own; I have often thought how little I should like to have to prove organic evolution in a court of law...**In spite of the activity in laboratories, direct proof of the derivation under natural circumstances of one form from another has still to be found. A sharp reminder that Evolution is still a theory that has never been proved by experiment...***[116]

(emphasis added)

The Holy Scripture requires two or three witnesses for the establishment of fact (Matthew 18:16). Thus it seems only reasonable to conclude that for whatever reasons given to explain why the knowledge base was relocated from Biblical absolutism to scientific naturalism, one of them is certainly not genuine scientific fact. I heard Ken Ham say recently that it is indeed "unbelievable what unbelievers have to believe in order to be unbelievers." [117]

THE KNOWLEDGE CHANGE BEGINS

In the midst of the thirteenth century (pre-Renaissance), a change in the ideological winds began to blow, and as amazing as it may seem, this change in wind direction (which was indeed the beginning of a paradigm shift), was originated in the organized church and was directed by the "sainted" Dominican, Thomas Aquinas. In this regard, Francis A. Schaeffer wrote:

> *He [Aquinas, 1225-1274], was the outstanding theologian of his day and his thinking is still dominant in some circles of the Roman*

Figure 3-d. Thomas Aquinas had a curious view of the fall of Adam.

> *Catholic Church...Aquinas held that man had revolted against God and thus was fallen, but Aquinas had an incomplete view of the Fall. He thought that the Fall did not affect man as a whole but only in part. In his view, the will was fallen or corrupted but the intellect was not affected.* **Thus people could rely on their own human wisdom, and this meant that people were free to mix the teaching of the Bible with the teaching of the non-Christian philosophers...** *Among the Greek philosophers Thomas Aquinas relied especially on one of the greatest, Aristotle (384-322 B.C.)... Aquinas managed to have Aristotle accepted, so that ancient non-Christian philosophy was re-enthroned.* [118] (emphasis added)

Along with Aquinas, other church leaders, political rulers, as well as the man on the street, also saw great significance in the literature, art, and ideas from the ancient Greek culture (800-300 B.C.). The ancient Greeks emphasized the importance of the individual and his life on earth. To give you a glimpse into things to come as the result of thirteenth century infatuation, particularly with the ancient Greeks, consider the salient remarks of History professor Edward N. Burns of Rutgers University:

> *Among all the peoples of the ancient world, the one whose culture most clearly exemplified the spirit of Western man was the hellenic or Greek. No other of these [ancient] nations had so strong a devotion to liberty, at least for itself, or so firm a belief in the nobility of human achievement.* **The Greeks glorified man as the most important creature in the universe** *and refused to submit to the dictation of priests or despots or even to humble themselves before their gods. Their*

> attitude was essentially secular and rationalistic; they exalted the spirit of free inquiry and made knowledge supreme over faith...At the end of the Dark Ages [in Greek history about 800 B.C.] the Greek was already well started along the road of social ideals that he was destined to follow in later centuries. He was an optimist convinced that life was worth living for its own sake, and he could see no reason for looking forward to death as a glad release. **He was an egoist, striving for the fulfillment of self.** As a consequence, he rejected mortification of the flesh and all forms of denial which would imply the frustrations of life. He could see no merit in humility of turning the other check. He was a humanist who worshiped the finite and the natural other than the worldly and the sublime. For this reason he refused to invest his gods with awe-inspiring qualities, or to invent any conception of man as a depraved or sinful creature. [119] (emphasis added)

Historically, therefore, this "new" thinking led to a period called the Renaissance and ultimately to the Enlightenment also. [120] It is easy to see that the Greek revival did not generate any new thinking at all; just the same old story that was told to our parents in Genesis 3:1-3.

THE RENAISSANCE AND THE RISE OF MODERN SCIENCE

Our present-day secularism in America, as well as the spiritual blight in the Church, can be traced, I believe, to the intellectual and spiritual departure from God and His Word that fructified as the result of the Italian Renaissance.

Figure 3-e. Chief among Darwin's talents, more than his scientific skills, was his ability to speculate endlessly.

Furthermore, I am convinced that the Renaissance, the Age of Reason (or what has been called the Enlightenment), and today's so-called "New Age" are nothing more than fancy names —surreptitious in design—that have been given to modern reoccurrences of the same rebellion of Genesis Three. In other words, the first historical reference of a Renaissance, the first Enlightenment, or the first "new age," actually took place when Satan convinced Eve that God didn't really mean what He had said concerning the "tree in the midst of the garden." Nevertheless, I am convinced that philosophical seeds were planted during the Renaissance that eventually made the present acceptance and dominance of Darwinian evolution inevitable.

To demonstrate the validity of these assertions, we must carefully consider the perceptions of this period (The Renaissance), that have been freely disbursed and believed in our present century. For example, historian Hutton Webster of the University of Nebraska affirms that modern science really arose during the period of artistic and intellectual revival known as the Renaissance. What do you suppose he meant by "modern science?" He wrote that during the Renaissance:

> *Investigators then began to hark back to the methods of observation and experimentation which the Greeks had begun and without which no genuine knowledge of nature is possible. There was a reason for this: the Renaissance rediscovered the ancient classics, especially those of Greece, and so made accessible to educated men all that the Greeks had learned about the natural world...The Greeks, who for sheer mental power have never been surpassed, did much more in science. We owe to them the foundation of astronomy, physics, botany, and zoology ...The Romans, for all their genius as soldiers, lawgivers, and governors, never paid much attention to science; they were content to take over what the Greeks had discovered without making many new discoveries of their own. Science was also neglected in Christian Europe until the latter part of the Middle Ages. Throughout most of the medieval period men's minds were fixed on the supernatural world rather than on the natural world about them.* [121]

While there is little disagreement that the Renaissance was indeed a spectacular time of revival and renewal, and while it is true that because of the Renaissance individual and Biblical freedoms had been won from the yoke of Roman religious oppression (which surely aided the rise of modern science); nevertheless, much of what Webster has affirmed is typical of the "Rationalist Myth" that has emaciated God's original design for American education, theology, law, etc. Furthermore, this same materialistic rationale ultimately inspired the shift in our cultural world view under which we presently live.

The above quotation by Webster is taken from a secondary school textbook (*Modern European Civilization*), that was first published in 1920 by Heath and Company—which enjoyed widespread distribution for much of two decades—and is a prime example of the subtle and gradual disparagement against the Bible and Christianity that was already beginning to filter down from the nonbelieving, materialistic, evolutionary colleges and universities. Darwinism, which had been floating on the periphery of the academic scene in Europe and America a full generation before the publication of *The Origin*, emerged in the 1860's and 1870's, and was accepted at the university level as scientific proof that there is no God. In the wake of this evolutionary revival there was a behind-the-scenes prompting by the "academic elite" to push the clergy out of the chairs of leadership within the colleges and universities founded by their churches. By 1902, the last of these Christian colleges succumbed to this pressure, (Princeton), and to this day the college/ university system in America is a secular operation with a deep evolutionary orientation. [122]

THE GREEK BASIS FOR THE SHIFT

Anyone who is serious about his faith in the Bible and his subsequent life in Christ needs only to consider a few salient factors regarding the anti-Biblical design of classical Greek thought and the true nature of Webster's specious comments (mentioned above), will come into clear focus. As a matter of fact, the Apostle Paul, at a place called "Mar's Hill,"* confronted vestiges

---

*Dr. Ralph Earle, *Word Meanings in the N.T.*, p. 114, writes: "Mar's Hill—the Greek expression is the same here as in verse 19, where it is properly translated AREOPAGUS. It is AREIOS PAGOS, (only two places in NT). ARES was the Greek name for Mars, the god of war—hence, "Mar's hill" (KJV). The supreme council of Athens met on this hill, and so was

of classical Greece while in Athens (Acts 17). As Paul was reasoning with the "Jews and the God-fearing Greeks" concerning the "good news about Jesus and the resurrection", there was a group of philosophers who confronted him—descendants of Aristotelian thinking (Epicureans and Stoics by name).* The point is that these two philosophical systems were fundamentally evolutionary systems as well as being Aristotelian. Dr. Louis T. More gave a series of lectures in 1925 at Princeton University in which he said:

> *After Aristotle's death, Greek thought gradually divided into the two schools of the Stoics and the Epicureans**...These two*

---

given the name Areopagus."

*Both the Stoics and the Epicureans were opposed to Christianity. Both systems of thought were materialistically monistic, i.e. they only believed "in the world of physical matter, with no nonmaterial entities existing of any kind that cannot in principal be incorporated into the realm of matter and its actions" (*Long War,* Morris, p. 212). Like Carl Sagan wrote, and all other evolutionists believe, matter is all there is—and it is the mother of us all! "Epicurus (342-270 B.C.) to some extent was a follower of Aristotle, who died when Epicurus was still a young man. However, Epicurus denied that there was any purposive force in nature. He believed in an infinite number of worlds, but no gods. Everything on earth had evolved directly from the earth material itself, according to Epicurus and his followers...Stoics, on the other hand, [established by Zeno in the late 300s B.C. in Athens] stressed the simple life and submission to whatever circumstances life might present. They believed in the beauty and orderliness of the world as an evidence of God, but their concept of God was purely pantheistic" (Morris, *Long War,* p. 212, 213). Dr. Morris, quoting Dr. Louis More, adds: "After endless and profitless circumlocution the Stoics reconcile the two antinomies [a contradiction between two apparently equally valid principles] by identifying God with the active force. The result is a pure pantheism in which matter is vitalized because God has implanted in it from the beginning a *ratio seminalis,* or rational seed. Having once made a start the cosmos develops according to natural law in succession of time" (Louis T. More, The Dogma of Evolution, p. 68; also cited in Morris, p. 213). This sounds strangely like the modern doctrine called Theistic Evolution to me, an anti-Biblical theory that many Christian theologians have embraced!

**In this connection one needs to take a look at Titus Lucretius Carus (98-55 B.C.). He was a Roman poet and an Epicurean whose most notable work was *De rerum natura* (The Nature of the Universe). The Latin preposition "De" connotes source, or ownership, or origin; thus the title can carry the idea that the universe is the source, origin and owner of nature or things. This poem was a lengthy didactic work consisting of six books, in which he gave an exposition of Epicurean philosophy. Among other anti-Biblical ideas, Lucretius

schools had the world of thought in allegiance well into the Roman Empire and exerted much influence on Christian writers, their ideas of science and evolution are very important. [123]

Figure 3-f. This is the title page from the 1743 copy of Lucretius' work *On the Nature of the Universe*.

Accordingly, any idea or notion originating in ancient Greece would essentially be pagan and evolutionary, and therefore anti-Biblical and anti-Christian. Whether or not it possessed any lasting scientific content or benefit becomes a matter for further

---

set forth the doctrine that the world developed from the chance processes caused by atoms moving through space. To him gods existed, but not to intervene in human affairs. Furthermore, he believed that all entities were material in origin—even the soul of man. Accordingly, for him the soul of man is not immortal. He wrote: "The world has persisted many long years, having once been set going in the appropriate motions. From these everything else follows...Bear this well in mind, and you will immediately perceive that nature is free and uncontrolled by proud masters and runs the universe by herself without the aid of gods." Reprinted in *Theories of the Universe*, Milton K. Munitz, ed. (Glencoe, IL, The Free Press, 1957), p. 53. Also cited in Morris, *The Long War*, p. 212.

question and study. I don't want to belabor this point, nevertheless, the documentation in this area is copious.* However, it is important to the thesis of this chapter, as well as to your insight into the true nature of Webster's comments, that I relate at least one of the more preeminent by-products that evolved from the Hellenic encroachment into early and medieval Christian thought.

Take note, "down to the close of the Middle Ages...questions of fact were settled not by experiment but by authority. Broadly speaking, authority in spiritual matters was represented by the Bible, while authority in what we would call scientific questions was represented by Aristotle." [124] However, it must be understood that the line of separation between these two disciplines was always blurred. One generation would have more of a Bible orientation, while another would be more Hellenic—the point is: Aristotle became thoroughly intertwined in the thinking of the Latin West, and especially in the Roman religious system (see Figure **3-g**).

The best illustration of this fact can be observed by the serious repercussions that resulted between the empirical scientists —Copernicus, Galileo, and company—and the philosophers and theologians of Rome. This most crucial confrontation was due to the advancements in sixteenth century astronomy.

Prior to the earthshaking work and theory of Nicolaus Copernicus (1473-1543 A.D.), the accepted cosmological view of the universe was called the geocentric view of the universe (that is, the earth was believed to be the center of the known universe and all other heavenly bodies were thought to revolve around the earth). Both Copernicus, and later Galileo Galilei (1564-1642 A.D.), took the opposing and unpopular view called the heliocentric view of the universe, which meant a sun-centered universe.

---

*For a thorough accounting of this particular topic read: Chapter One of *The Bible in the Age of Science*, by Dr. Alan Richardson (SCM Press LTD, London.) 1961.

In this view the earth, as well as the other heavenly bodies, were believed to orbit the sun. As you may be aware, this debate was of considerable importance because even to this very day skeptics charge the Roman church of the Middle Ages with the pseudoscientific notion of geocentricism.* This, of course, the Roman church believed. The greater damage was done because Galileo's critics also purported that this idea is of Scriptural origin. Therefore it is concluded that this is a case showing the Bible to be scientifically unreliable. However, what you may not be aware of is that, while the earth is indeed the spiritual center of the universe, the Bible does not present a geocentric view of the solar system. [125]

Figure **3-g**. Aristotle, (384-322 B.C.) The Father of Modern Rationalism.

---

*The geocentric theory was further strengthened and popularized by Ptolemy of Alexander (100?-170? A.D.).

The reason for the difficulty was due to the veneration that had developed in the Roman religious system for Aristotelian cosmology. I have already spoken of Aristotle's influence brought to the thirteenth century church by Thomas Aquinas (1225-1274 A.D.); however, Dr. Alan Richardson, of the University of Nottingham, makes the following validatory comments:

> *So well had Aquinas succeeded in Christianizing Aristotle that when the authority of Aristotle in the sphere of astronomy or physics was called into question, it seemed as though Christian truth itself was being impiously assailed. So completely had Aristotle and the Bible been harmonized in the medieval synthesis of natural and revealed theology that the overthrow of Aristotelian philosophy by the rise of modern science seemed to the Aristotelian philosophers, [many of whom were Roman Theologians], though not to the new scientists themselves, to involve the rejection of the Biblical revelation as well."* [126]

The dilemma was due to the nature of "Greek science." In order to know a little more about "Greek science," and more specifically Aristotle, I need to say a word about Plato (see Figure **3-h**). Plato (429-347 B.C.), whose real name was Aristotcles and who was Aristotle's mentor, "conceived reality itself as consisting of pure Ideas which were knowable not by the senses but only by *theoria*, intellectual contemplation." [127]

By the way, I think it is interesting that our English term theory is derived from this same Greek word. Furthermore, if you will carefully consider Plato's usage of the word theory (intellectual contemplation), I think you can see a significant similarity regarding the way the word theory has been applied to modern evolutionism.

Figure 3-h.

Aristotle departed to some degree from Plato in that he believed the content of ideas must be known through observation and not just mentally contrived, for "he was...a shrewd and careful observer of nature." [128] Therefore to Aristotle, as with most Greeks, nature existed in mathematical forms that could be understood in mathematical constructs. He, therefore, hypothetically/deduced that the earth was the center of many celestial circles (geocentric). These circles were to him a series of concentric crystal spheres in which the stars (he thought to be animate beings), were set. Quite simply, the method of "Greek Science" is deductive reasoning based on assumption alone. It was void of any experimental support. Dr. Richardson explains it perfectly:

If one is convinced that the pure rational form is the circle [as did Aristotle]...then one will

tend to regard any appearance of elliptical movements in nature, [the shape of the earth's orbit as discovered by Kepler based on telescopic observation], as an error of human observation, **since we tend to see only what we are convinced must be there; we look for evidence which will confirm our a priori [deductive] conceptions and simply do not see things which do not conform to them.** [129]
(emphasis added)

Thus we see that the true nature of knowledge about reality hasn't changed much; like I said in Chapter One—one's paradigm controls what one believes, and what one believes influences what one sees—and around and around we go. Aristotle and the ancient Greeks were certainly no exception to this rule. Even Aristotle said, "It is not the facts which divide men but the interpretation of the facts." [130] The Bible puts it just like it is, and by doing so, it clearly explains Aristotle's statement: *"AS A MAN THINKS IN HIS HEART SO IS HE"* (Proverbs 23:7).

HELIOCENTRIC VIEW VS. GEOCENTRIC VIEW

The real problem between Galileo and the Roman church had nothing to do with the Bible, but rather the deeply entrenched Aristotelian cosmology and those who believed it. The battle was not religion versus science as is generally reported by skeptics today. As I have already told you, the new scientists were men like Copernicus, Galileo, Kepler, Newton, Linnaeus, John Ray, etc., and scores of others, all of whom were devout students of the Bible and committed believers in Christ. Accordingly, Galileo's crime,* if indeed he committed one, was that he challenged the

---

*GALILEO GALILEI (1564-1642) followed the heliocentric Copernican theory of astronomy and published his famous *A Dialogue on the Two Principal Systems of the World* (1632). It is somewhat ironic that he published this highly controversial volume for two reasons.

security of officialdom; "his teaching was an attack upon the establishment."[131] Dr. Richardson indicates that:

> *The struggle of the new scientists against the old order was not a struggle of "science" against "religion" but the revolt of the new scientific philosophy against the old Aristotelian pseudoscientific philosophy.*[132]

Accordingly, a "Rationalist Myth" was developed and has been propagated among the learned to this very day (which is also the essence the earlier statement of Hutton Webster—see page 107). This myth asserts that:

> *The men of science [during] the Renaissance, with the rekindled lights of Hellas [Ancient Greece] shining in their faces, courageously withstood the entrenched arrogance of ecclesiastical dogmatism, and, amidst the fanatical religious wars and persecutions of the sixteenth and seventeenth centuries, began the great assault upon the tyranny of religion and ignorance...* **Greek science was not**

First, it was a deliberate refutation of the Aristotelian geocentric cosmology; and second he had already been censored by the church (1616) about his Copernican views and had promised not to teach them anymore. Nevertheless, he presented his views as a *Dialogue* between three participants: Salviati—a Copernican, Sagredo—a Ptolemaic astronomer, and Simplicius—a stupid Aristotelian philosopher. As the result, he was summoned to appear before the Roman Inquisition of ten judges. He appeared on June 21, 1633. Hummel said, "His trial has been held up as the prime example of Christianity's hostility to free inquiry and to scientific progress...But was the conflict so clear-cut? Whose system did Galileo set out to disrupt, the religious authority of Rome or the scientific authority of Aristotle?" *The Galileo Connection* (Intervarsity Press: Downers Grove, Il. 60515, 1986), p. 13. Galileo said, "The Bible tells us how to go to Heaven, not how the heavens go..." (Ibid. p. 9). Legend has it that after recanting of his views that the earth moves before the Inquisition, he murmured under his breath: "E pur si muove." That is, "But is does move!" For an excellent account: see G. de Santillana. *The Crime of Galileo* (London, 1958); also, Charles E. Hummel. *The Galileo Connection.*

Figure 3-i. Nicholas Copernicus (1473-1543), denied that the earth was the physical center of the solar system thus discrediting the long standing theories of Ptolemy.

Figure 3-j. Galileo Galilei (1564-1642), confirmed the views of Nicholas Copernicus that the sun was the center of the solar system as the true biblical position even though the Roman theologians of his day could not accept his position.

the inspiration of the modern scientific movement; it had to be demolished and a new start had to be made before the modern science could begin.

The "Myth" does less than justice to Galileo and his fellow pioneers, because it minimizes the magnitude of their accomplishments. ***They were not in fact taking up a quest which the ancient Greeks had been forced to lay down; they were starting an entirely new venture of the human spirit.*** [133] (emphasis added)

Figure 3-k. Ptolemy (85-165 A.D.), taught that the heavens were made of crystalline spheres and that the earth was in the center of this system. The Roman church used this view of the solar system until it was refuted by Copernicus and Galileo.

The popularity of this "myth" the last century or so, is due to an unparalleled wonderment for ancient Greece, and paganism in general, among the history, science, and theological professors of America and Western Europe. As Otto Scott, a brilliant Christian historian intimated:

> *We have been fed a diet of fingernails, fingernail polish, hairdye, wigs, and shoulderstraps in the name of history. The professors and textbooks begin with Egypt; they quickly move to pagan Greece and Rome; touch lightly the Middle Ages, and then go straight to the Renaissance and the Enlightenment. At the end of the class, we have nothing from which to form our opinions and images of history but the hem of the historical garment.* [134]

THE CENSORSHIP OF REAL HISTORY

The body and soul of the history of Western thought has been, and is still being, ignored by modern scholarship—and this is the epitome of censorship! If Christianity is left out of our consideration concerning the development of Western Civilization, we are looking at nothing but the shell of human thought and experience. What's been left out? The overwhelming influence of the Hebrew-Christian ethic—that's what has been left out! By the way, it's still being left out (see Figure 3-1)! **This fact has been overwhelmingly proved by Dr. Paul Vitz in his remarkable book *Censorship: Evidence of Bias in our Children's Textbooks*** (which of course carries over into high school and college). Dr. Vitz's work is a 680 page short-form of a report from the Department of Education. This work was the result of a study that was conducted by several researchers, who, in the 1980's investigated 60 top history textbooks that were being used by nearly 90% of our nation's school children.

The purpose of the study was to determine how the traditional beliefs of America were being presented. Dr. Vitz plainly reported that:

> *...**bias** is primarily accomplished by **exclusion**, by leaving out...such a bias is much harder to observe than a positive vilification or direct criticism, but it is the essence of censorship. It is effective not only because it's hard to observe—it isn't there—and therefore hard to counteract.* [135] (emphasis added)

Commenting on this same report, Charles Krauthammer wrote in an article that was printed in the *Washington Post Magazine*, that:

> *...It is true that school textbooks have recently developed an allergy to traditional religion. Like blacks a generation ago, religion hardly exists in the world of **Dick and Jane**. Paul Vitz, a professor at New York University, plowed heroically through 60 social science textbooks and shows that they **grossly ignore** the role of religion...[i.e. Christianity] in American history and society. One textbook manages to give the Pilgrims thirty pages without once trespassing on the issue of the religious [Christian] motivation for their excursion to the new World. Another text defines Pilgrim as "people who make long trips.* [136]

Why does this happen? The answer lies I believe, in the words of liberal thinker and writer, Jeremy Rifkin:

> *Evolutionary theory has been enshrined as the centerpiece of our educational system, and*

elaborate walls have been erected around it to protect it from unnecessary abuse. [137]

Thus it is that the mere worship of the Greeks and Romans continues to hypnotize the professors. As did Webster in the above quote by him (p. 107), they seem to fasten an admiring gaze on what J. C. Stobart called *The Glory That Was Greece* [138] and *The Grandeur that Was Rome*. [139] What about this "Glory" and this "Grandeur"? Otto Scott said:

> *Much is made of the inventions of the Greeks—where the first steam engine was produced; where heated floors appeared; where techniques of leverage were applied; where theoretical mathematics were discussed, etc. [However] much less is said about Maculey's observation that the proud slave owners of Greece spurned the use of all those inventions, because to them all their innovations did was to relieve the labor of the slaves. The slave owners themselves never labored and therefore didn't need such comforts.*
>
> *Still less is said about the unwanted infants that were left out in the open for wild dogs to eat; about the complete lack of medical facilities for the poor; the absence of orphanages, etc.—about the Roman games where first animals and then people were put to death for entertainment—about the human sacrifices to gods and goddesses—about the rampant immorality and fleshly indulgence—That was The Grandeur That Was Greece and The Glory That Was Rome.* [140]

The point is—ancient Greek philosophy and modern scientific advancements have come to be seen as natural compliments of each other. This is obviously not true! What is true, however, is that modern scholarship has chosen a secularized form of knowledge and ancient Greece provides them their apparent legitimacy.

Figure 3-I. Humanistic educators have erased our Christian History subtly but effectively.

Modern science—that is, real science—was indeed produced by men who followed the reasonability of a Creator, who, they believed, had designed law and order in nature and natural processes. Such was this law and order, they felt, that it could be followed and examined. As Johann Kepler said they were "thinking God's thoughts after Him." [141] These great men of science, a list of which can be found in Appendix C, found absolutely no discord between science and the Bible. As a matter of fact, Newton himself spent many long hours with the Bible. Furthermore, it is generally agreed that Newton's famous work *Philosphie Naturalis Principia Mathaematica* (Mathematical Principles of Natural Philosophy)—in which he discusses the systems of the world based on his newly derived laws of motion and gravity—was a scientific commentary of Psalms 19: "The heavens declare the glory of God, and the firmament showeth His handiwork." [142] Moreover, many of these great scientists were humble, witnessing Christians—as Robert Boyle (1627-1691)—who was one of the founders of the famous Royal Society of London and father of modern chemistry. He was profoundly interested in [Christian] missions and devoted much of his money to Bible translation and the propagation of the gospel". [143]

Figure 3-m. Isaac Newton (1642-1727), was without a doubt one of the greatest scientists of the modern era. Contrary to popular belief, his gifted intellect did not distract from his ardent belief in Jesus Christ as his savior and the Bible as God's eternal word.

In the same regard, the famous Blaise Pascal (1623-1662—Blaz Pas' kal'), an exceptionally brilliant French scientist and philosopher, whose mathematical acumen paved the way for the development of differential calculus. His life and attitude was a beautiful portrayal of the vital affinity between faith and science. He took the Aristotelian thinkers to task and without question openly legitimatized the newly developed scientific method as the only way to ascertain truth in physics. Above all, "Pascal's authority became the Holy Scripture..." [144] Charles E. Hummel, while reflecting on Pascal's commitment to Christianity, writes:

> On the night of November 23, 1654, Pascal had an intense, two-hour religious experience which he recorded and kept secret. For eight years he took care to sew and unsew it in the lining each time he changed his coat. His Memorial was discovered a few days after his death:
>
> FIRE
>
> God of Abraham, God of Isaac,
> God of Jacob, not of the philosophers and scholars. Certitude. Certitude. Feeling, Joy, Peace.
> God of Jesus Christ,
> My God and thy God.
> "Thy God shall be my God."
> Forgetfulness of the world and of everything except God.
> His is to be found only by the ways taught in the Gospel.
> Greatness of the soul of man.
> "Righteous Father, the world hath not known thee,
> But I have known Thee."
> Joy, joy, joy, tears of joy.

> *Jesus Christ.*
> *I have fallen away: I have fled from Him, denied Him, crucified Him.*
> *May I not fall away forever.*
> *We keep hold of Him only by the ways taught in the Gospel.*
> *Renunciation, total and sweet.*
> *Total submission to Jesus Christ and to my director.*
> *Eternally in joy for a day's exercise on earth.*
> *I will not forget Thy word. AMEN.* [145]

I trust that these brief words have cast sufficient light on the true nature of the Greek-based Renaissance, as well as the deceptive attempts by nonbelieving, materialistic historians and educators (as Hutton Webster and others), who have attempted to alienate the Bible from genuine science. Sadly, in the estimation of a great many Americans, they have succeeded. We will later learn that eighteenth, nineteenth, and twentieth century scientists, philosophers, and even theologians, returned to Aristotle's hypothetico/deductive method in their justification of evolutionism. In other words, they hypothetically developed a theory or an idea about first origins and total reality, which obviously fits their world view. Then they have deduced endlessly from their assumptions about first origins to this very day, while inventing speculative evidence to prove their wild assumptions. This is how evolution achieved "scientific" status? This great deception occurred because they said that their findings had been achieved by the scientific method (inductive reasoning, i.e. facts to theory)—same method used legitimately by Newton, Kepler, Galileo and others. Of course, this is a big joke, but this kind of thinking sheds light on Paul's warning to Timothy: "...keep that which is committed to thy trust, **avoiding profane and vain babblings, and oppositions of science falsely so-called**: which some professing have erred concerning the faith. Grace be with thee. Amen" (I Timothy 6:20-21, KJV).

THE RENAISSANCE: A DEEPER LOOK

The Renaissance (a French word meaning *rebirth or revival*), was a time in Western Europe (1300 A.D. to 1650 A.D.), that saw a renewed interest in the ancient Greco-Roman classics, philosophy, and style. Consequently, the paganism of the ancients was added to the already diluted Christian rationale. Thus the philosophical door was opened in Western thought for a deep and thorough defection from all Biblical roots. This is not to say that the mind-set of Western Europe before the Renaissance was a haven of Biblical Christianity. Quite far from it! It is a well documented fact that soon after the beginning of the second century, Western Christian thought began to mix with Classical Greek thought. Furthermore, the work of the Scholastics* had already skillfully interwoven Greek thought into Christian theological exposition. Thomas Aquinas, who is called the supreme master of the Scholastic system, as we have already stated, invited Aristotelian realism into Christian thought, while other churchmen had done the same for Platonic idealism (namely, the Dominicans and the Franciscans, respectively).[146] Even though the Scholastics maintained that the Bible was, in fact, a divine revelation, their mixture of truth with paganism proved to be disastrous, as is witnessed by the Biblical departures of the Renaissance.

---

*SCHOLASTICS—this term refers to a group of churchmen, generally Roman Catholic, who embraced a system of philosophy and theology (Scholasticism) that applied the ideas of non-Christians (especially Plato and Aristotle) to matters of the Christian faith. It was their hope that a synthesis between faith, reason, and knowledge could be achieved. Some historians date the beginnings of Scholasticism all the way back to St. Paul and St. Peter, while others indicate that it was unique to the 12th and 13th centuries. However, it seems that the Apostle Paul did warn the church about such dangers (as per Colossians 2:8, e.g. Gnosticism). This chronological argument dealing with the time these departures (mixtures) took place is not that important. What is important is that this mixture happened and it is affecting our world view and faith today.

The primary evil that surfaced during the Renaissance, which became the fountainhead from which emanated many other secondary evils, was the open disparagement of the Bible. Rousas John Rushdoomy penned in his incomparable *The Institutes of Biblical Law* that:

> *The Renaissance unleashed a great flood of violence by its hostility to godly law.* [147]

Some may argue that the revolt was aimed at the superstitions and authority of the Roman religious system and not the Bible at all. To a degree this is true, but the sad fact is the Bible was inseparably associated with the religion of the middle ages (the period some have called the Dark Ages), and was discredited along with the rest of the Roman system. Dr. Earle E. Cairns made this noteworthy comment:

> *In the broader sense the Renaissance may be defined as that era of cultural reorientation in which men substituted a modern secular individualistic view of life for the medieval religious corporate approach to life...The medieval theocentric conception of the world, in which God was the measure of all things, gave way to an anthropocentric [man centered] view of life, in which man became the measure of all things.* [148]

So we see as God and His word was systematically replaced by man and his reason, the way was prepared for the rise of all sorts of evil. Among the many secondary evils that could be listed, there are two that are important to the meaning of this Chapter. The first one, and one that is implicit within the above quote by

Dr. Cairns, is the unnatural ascension of man to the center of all existence. Dr. V. H. H. Green wrote that during the Renaissance:

> *There was an increasing faith in the possibilities of the human will. The Renaissance concept of individuality, rooted in the idea of the greatness and uniqueness of man, naturally implies his liberty.* [149]

The humanism of the Renaissance therefore was set on freeing man from the bondage of what was considered medieval ignorance. The church* was ultimately blamed with the perpetuation of this ignorance, and we must remember that the Bible, since it was considered the church's charter, ultimately received the greater condemnation. Eventually, as the scientific age became more and more materialistic the Bible was looked upon as a book of silly superstitions.

To accomplish the deliverance of the individual, the Renaissance scholars emphasized a well-rounded education. History is replete with examples showing that education is always a tool that is successfully used for effecting change in a culture. Accordingly, it was recorded in one history textbook that students of this period were admonished to:

> *...take care [and]...Add a little every day and gather things in. Remember that these studies promise you enormous prizes both in the conduct of your life and the fame and glory of your name...acquaint yourself with what per-*

---

*Throughout this brief section of medieval and Renaissance history, when I refer to the "church," it is the apostate Roman religious system that is in view.

> *tains to life and manners—those things that are called humane studies because they perfect and adorn man.* [150]

Adorn who? Why? So it was, that more and more literature and philosophy (especially Hellenic), was taught during this period.[151] Thus the Bible became a significantly small influence in the lives of a growing number of Western Europeans. Man became the center and cause for all educational processes, not to make him a better disciple of Christ, but rather to elevate his knowledge so that he could become self-sufficient, famous, and successful.

THE RENAISSANCE AND ARISTOTLE

An example of the content of Renaissance teaching, and to better illustrate the lasting effects (and there were many), of ancient Greek thought that were revived during the Renaissance, the renewal of Aristotle's *Scala Naturae* (The Great Chain of Being), is a prime example, especially for our present study. It was Aristotle's thinking, though not unique with him, that nature was existent in a continuous graduated order. The fact that Aristotle was used by the Renaissance Fathers as their source of Greek philosophy (i.e. materialistic rationalism and naturalism—the essential substance of evolutionism), must not be used as an indication that he originated this system of thought. Because he did not! What he did was organize and articulate this system of rationale better than any other of his predecessors. As a matter of fact, Dr. Henry M. Morris traces its origin all the way back to Nimrod who was taught it by Satan himself.[152]

In Greek history evolutionary materialism can easily be seen all the way back in the Milesian School (a school in the Ionian city of Miletus—sixth century B.C.), and was associated with men like Thales, Anaximander, and Anaximenes. By the end of the sixth century B.C. with the development of a more metaphysical turn in Greek thought, Pythagoras and his followers, called the Pythagoreans, intensified their concern about the nature of the universe. Ultimately a strong materialism emerged from their debates that was expressed by Heracleitus. He viewed the universe as constantly changing. Therefore, "evolution or constant change [was seen to be] the law of the universe...[and] no underlying substance exists immutable through all eternity." [153]

Figure 3-n. Democritus (460?-357? B.C.), was a pre-Socratic Greek philosopher and is considered to be the most consistent materialist in the history of Greek thought.

In the latter half of the fifth century B.C. the famous Democritus, the man given credit for the development of the atomic theory, provided the final details in the formulation of Greek materialism. Democritus and his cohorts are called atomists because of their work on the atomic theory. As such, they believed that the universe is made up of atoms, "infinite in number, indestructible, and indivisible." [154] From this conclusion it was a simple step to the notion that every single object in the universe was produced randomly by chance relationships between atoms, which is the essence of materialistic thought.

As Greece reached her Golden Age (4th & 5th century B.C.), Athens also achieved an advanced state of democracy. During this time there arose in Athens a group of philosophers called Sophists, who spoke plainly on these matters. The chief spokesman for the Sophist school was Protagoras. Protagoras did most of his teaching in Athens and is known for his famous dictum, "Man is the measure of all things," which epitomizes the fullness of Sophist philosophy. [155] From this basis Protagoras taught that "[1] Goodness, truth, justice, and beauty are relative to the needs and interests of man himself. [2] There are no absolute truths or eternal standards of right and justice. [3] The sense perception, [empirical observation], is the exclusive source of knowledge. [4] Morality likewise varies from one people to another." [156] The work of Protagoras put the final plank into the coffin lid of organized secular thought that would eventually produce Darwinian evolutionism.

The fourth century B.C. saw the coming of both Socrates and Plato both of whom disputed the relativism, skepticism, and the individualism of the Sophists. Aristotle, a student of Plato, followed Plato's teaching for a brief while, however, he eventually fell out with Platonic idealism and reverted to a pro-Sophist mindset. Aristotle saw all matter, both living and nonliving, ascending on a ladder, rising step at a time, from inanimate matter all the way up to the creative force. "This concept [The Great Chain of Being], can be traced back to Plato, but it was especially popular from the Renaissance on through the eighteenth century and finds modern expression in Darwinian evolutionism." [157] As such, this idea presented the eighteenth and nineteenth century scientists with a "monumentally static picture of nature." [158] This idea was conceptualized by them under the above rubric—The Great *Chain of Being*. The late Loren Eiseley, Professor of Anthropology and History of Science at the University of Pennsylvania, openly admitted that:

> *All that the Chain of Being actually needed to become a full-fledged evolutionary theory was the introduction into it of the conception of time in vast quantities added to mutability of form. It demanded, in other words, a universe not made but being made continuously...As we look back upon the long reign of the Scale of Being, whose effects, as we shall see, persisted well into the nineteenth century, we may observe that the **seed of evolution** lay buried in this traditional metaphysic which indeed prepared the Western mind for its acceptance.* [159] (emphasis added)

Furthermore, it is of equal importance to our study to know that Aristotle incorporated within his scheme (Scala Naturae), a certain deification of nature. This, of course, is exactly what Darwin did with his evolutionary mechanism that he called *natural selection*. Ian Taylor indicated that:

> *Aristotle...found it difficult to believe that a single great intelligence could direct every day-to-day detail. He reasoned that the Creator had given to every living thing, even to individual organs, a teleological principle or built-in purpose, so that throughout all time each organ would develop according to plan...By ascribing a purpose to nature, Aris-*

> totle gave nature a characteristic of deity, and, in a subtle way, this has tended to redirect men's attention towards the complete personification and even deification of nature itself. The historian Hooykaas (1972), has shown that Charles Darwin continually personified nature with remarks such as, "natural selection picks out with unerring skill the best varieties" (p. 18). [160]

As such, it was believed (and still is), that the ultimate task of natural selection was to bring man to his present estate—perfected by natural processes at the top of the chain!

The second of these ancillary evils which discernibly figured into the overthrow of the Biblical knowledge base for total reality in Western thought, was the tendency of Renaissance scholarship to equalize all religions. This clearly necessitated the demotion of Christianity, which in turn promoted all other religious systems. You will note that a pattern is being followed. One that will again surface in both the nineteenth and twentieth centuries. First the Bible is discredited and then, as a natural consequence, the system of faith supported by the Bible—*Biblical Christianity*. Dr. Roland H. Bainton, Professor of Ecclesiastical History at Yale, wrote:

> The religion of the Renaissance was very hospitable to a universal deism in which Christianity retained a nominal headship chiefly because already sublimated and transformed without any conscious attempt to abandon the faith. Renaissance mystics, notably the leaders of the Neoplatonic Academy at Florence, sought to discover the same set of truths beneath the symbols of many systems: in the lore of Zoroaster, the mysteries of the divine

> *Hermes Trismegistus, in the alluring number speculations of the Jewish cabala. In such circles there were dreams of the reunion of all Christendom and even of a World Parliament of Religion.* **Tolerance** *became the watchword even at the expense of an emasculated Christianity.* [161] (emphasis added)

The Renaissance, then, was the forerunner to the incredibly broad and sweeping changes that were soon to land on the all shores of Western Europe. These changes would transform the knowledge base from a Biblical orientation to one based on human reason alone—the effects of this change would prove devastating!

A Little About The Reformation

As we pass though this period of European history in our attempt to present the foundational causes for today's affinity to evolutionism, I would be remiss if I did not, at least briefly, discuss the Reformation (16th Century). The Renaissance had provided the individual liberty for the common man to think on his own, as well as the freedom to express his thoughts. In addition to this, there was the added ability to mass produce literature in one's own language (the Bible included), as the result of the invention of the Gutenberg press. Thus by the beginning of the sixteenth century there was an intellectual and a spiritual climate in Western Europe that could no longer tolerate the unscriptural teachings or the heathen practices of the Roman religious system. Dr. Cairns articulates distinctly in this regard:

> *The intellectual changes wrought by the Renaissance ...created an intellectual outlook that favored the development of Protestantism. The desire to return to sources of the*

past led the Christian Humanists* of the north to a study of the Bible in the original tongues of the Scriptures. Thus the difference between the Church of the New Testament and the medieval Roman Catholic Church became clear to them, and this difference was to the disadvantage of the medieval papal ecclesiastical organization. Renaissance emphasis upon the individual was a helpful factor in the development of the Protestant insistence that salvation was a personal matter to be settled by the individual...The critical spirit of the Renaissance was used by the Reformers to justify observation of the hierarchy and sacraments of the medieval Roman church and a critical comparison of them with the Scriptures...Though the Renaissance in Italy proceeded along humanistic and pagan lines, the tendencies that it fostered were taken over in Northern Europe by the Christian Humanists and the Reformers and used by them to justify individual study of the Bible in the original as the source document of the Christian faith. [162] (emphasis added)

Dr. Robert A. Baker adds:

One of the greatest antecedents of reform was the movement known as the Renaissance. The throbbing of new intellectual life

---

*CHRISTIAN HUMANISTS—It would seem that the word Christian and humanist are contradictory terms. They are, if the brand of humanism in question is secular, materialistic, and evolutionary. However the two terms can be legitimately married in the context of Mark 12:30, that is, one can be a Christian humanist if he sees man as created in the image of God, and serves man as an outgrowth of his love (agape) for the eternal Creator and Savior.

and the discovery of new worlds profoundly prepared the way for reformation. [163]

It seems as if God in His everlasting mercy, knowing the extremes of atheism and infidelity (to which the philosophical course of the Renaissance would finally attain), not only used the Reformers to draw attention to the holy Scriptures as the only basis for truth about all reality, but He also permitted them to righteously use their newly gained personal freedom to warn the Western world concerning the inevitable results of their present course. To illustrate this aspect of the Reformation, consider the following episode taken from the life of Martin Luther (see Figure 3-o):

Luther's first challenge in the great task of Reformation came in October, 1517, when Monk Tetzel falsely accused him of selling indulgences. Antagonism between these two monks deepened as Luther gave the lie of Tetzel's untrue statements by writing so strongly against Romanist practices. On December 10, 1520, the then Pope issued a bull [a written papal edict], forbidding Luther to continue in his protestations; but, amid a large crowd of people gathered at the Elster Gate at Wittenburg, he burned the bull. When he went out to meet the Pope's legate at Augsburg his fellow citizens who loved him watched him as, in his monk's brown frock, he walked out to the gates. They cried, "Luther forever!" **He replied, "Nay, Christ forever! All wisdom of the world is childish foolishness compared with an acknowledgement of Christ."** [164] (emphasis added)

Thus as always: *"...Where sin abounded, grace did much more abound"* (Romans 5:20). Alas, as history consistently reports that the warnings of God are ignored by men—and so history once again confirms this sad fact. The rapid apostasy of Renaissance humanism was somewhat decelerated as the result of the Reformation (1517-1650), however, this interruption was soon removed. When Luther, Calvin, Knox, etc. were gone, their righteous use of the individual freedoms, all of which were restored as a result of the Renaissance, soon became secularized. This reminds me of an episode explained in Judges 2:10: "And also all that generation [Joshua and the elders of Israel] were gathered unto their fathers: and there arose another generation after them which knew not the **LORD**, nor the works which he had done for Israel." (KJV) Dr. Lindsell makes this timely comment:

> *The Reformation changed the educational patterns of Europe permanently. Education had been a church function and it was controlled by the Catholics everywhere...the great universities served as an arm of the church for the education of the clergy. There was no such thing as secular education. All of this was to change as the Reformation opened the door wide for the establishment of educational institutions by different Protestant churches.* **And this in turn was to lead sooner or later to secular education divorced from any church...**Once the Protestant churches claimed their **freedom** *to dissent and* **freedom** *to believe other than what was taught by Rome,* **they opened the doors to wider dissent and to irreligion as well.** *If the Protestant churches had the right to disagree with Rome, then the people of those communities also had the right to dissent from the Protestant teachings.* **Religious freedom carried with it the risk that**

*people could become anything they chose to become--adherents to the ethnic religions or any of a variety of new sects that came into being, **skeptics, or even atheists**. Moreover the very notion of religious freedom of necessity included the right to disseminate and to propagate religious ideas of every sort, whether they were in accord with community standards or not. **This dangerous precedent had its roots in the Reformation and was to bring forth its own fruit in the years ahead.*** [165] (emphasis added)

Figure 3-o. Martin Luther (1483-1546), the monk who refused to be silent.

While the Reformation Fathers were by no means perfect, they nevertheless used the freedom of the Renaissance to break with Rome. Therefore they cannot be blamed for the secularism and skepticism that was soon to follow. Biblical humanism always declines to its secular expression when man removes God and His word from serious consideration. This declension in the righteous use of humanistic behavior is simply another case in point that demonstrates the bent that is given to one's lifestyle by one's world view. Dr. George P. Fisher, Professor of Ecclesiastical History at Yale University, presents the following lucid commentary of this terrible declension:

> *A brief historical review will show that the Reformation is not responsible for tendencies to skepticism and unbelief which have revealed themselves in modern society.* **These tendencies discovered themselves before Protestantism appeared. The Renaissance in Italy was skeptical in its spirit...** *Among the adherents of the Reformation in the seventeenth century a* **new scholasticism arose.** *A new* **yoke** *was imposed, hardly less onerous [that is, burdensome], than that which the Reformation had cast off.*
>
> *Hence there ensued a revolt, an extensive reaction, in behalf of this negative principle of opposition to human authority in religious concerns. Such a reaction, in the absence of an adequate check, was pushed to an extreme;* **so that the positive, or religious element of Protestantism was sacrificed. The cause of liberty of thought became identified with doubt or disbelief.** *Modern unbelief first*

took the form of Deism* which spread in Europe until it became the fashionable religion of the eighteenth century. In England, the wearisome conflict of theological parities impelled some to explore for a fundamental religion underlying these differences, for a creed which was held by all in common. **This contributed to the rise of Free-thinking, or Deism.** *It found the most congenial home in* **France,** *whence it spread among other nations,* **which then looked to France for their opinions as well as their manners and fashion...**Pantheism** *was a second legitimate step in the same path. It is the denial of the supernatural altogether; it merges the Creator in the creation, or rather in nature, which is considered the manifestation of an impersonal force or law. These types of unbelief affected the Catholic and Protestant nations alike. France, Catholic France, was the principal center of skepticism in the last century... Deism, and finally Materialism and Atheism, became the creed of the philosophers and of the educated class.* [166] (emphasis added)

---

*DEISM—a rationalistic movement of the 17th and 18th centuries whose adherents generally subscribed to a natural religion based on human reason and morality, and the belief in one God who, after creating the world and the laws governing it refrained from interfering with the operation of those laws, and on the rejection of every kind of supernatural intervention in human affairs, it not only allowed men to deny the authority of the church, but it also gave them doctrinal ground to deny all revealed truth. It was essentially atheistic in nature.

**PANTHEISM—a dominant belief of ancient Greece, which was reintroduced during the Renaissance. The major teaching of Pantheism stated that God was everything and everything was god. This is an extremely strong evolutionary stance that was condemned of the Apostle Paul (Romans 1:23-25).

How quickly the evil one can take advantage of even the wisest of men. Even while God was restoring truth to the church, the devil was planting the seeds for this present day translation of the Mystery of Iniquity—that is, materialistic, atheistic, new-age, evolutionism.

The Congealing Force Of The Enlightenment

The decisive product of the Renaissance was the depreciation of the Bible and the development of a "new" rationale with which to view the world. The world came to be viewed quite naturally and mechanistically so that all phenomena was explained by the so-called laws of nature—laws that could operate successfully without God. Thus as the Bible became less acceptable as the source for real knowledge, elusive and mythological forces such as the one called "mother nature" were contrived to replace the God of Scripture as the explanation for the development of matter and life (see Figure **3-p**). It is true that the free thinking and humanism of the Renaissance led men away from the medieval bondage of the Roman Church. As men became free from these old restraints, for the first time in centuries having the Bible in their own language, they began to see the Word of God afresh. However, as always, the pendulum of history never remains constant, nor can man ever be consistent. So the beauty of Reformational truth was soon lost in the confusion wrought by secularized protestantism, and as sad as it is true, the secularization of the Reformation seeded the Enlightenment.

The peoples of Western Europe during the eighteenth century identified this hundred year period as an **Age of Enlightenment**. It is thusly named because men had come to feel they could apply the scientific method along with their reason, and could as a result logically discover truth. This distinguishable characteristic of the Enlightenment, better known as rationalism, was the conviction held by such men as d'Alembert, Diderot, Rousseau, Voltaire, and many other famous names that could be mentioned. In one way or another, these men believed that truth could be attained solely by human reason. It is because of this cardinal faith among Enlightenment philosophe's* that historians also referred to this time as the Age of Reason.

Peter Gay, Professor of History at Yale, in his award winning book *The Enlightenment: An Interpretation*, categorically substantiates the progressive nature of the deterioration wrought upon the Hebrew-Christian ethic among Western thinkers as an outgrowth of the Renaissance and the Enlightenment. He writes:

> *The four centuries between 1300 and 1700 are the prehistory of the Enlightenment... These were the centuries that supplied the Enlightenment with its image of the past, both pagan and Christian, its vocabulary, its philosophical method, and much of its program... all the resistance of Christian institutions and all the tenacious hold of **religious belief did not prevent the resurgence of an old, and eventually the triumph of a new mode of thinking.** These were centuries when secular forces first expanded and then exploded whatever unity the Christian millennium had possessed. **It was the era of pagan Christianity.** [167]* (emphasis added)

---

*PHILOSOPHE—the French term for philosopher. Remember much of the atheistic tendency of the Enlightenment received its impetus from philosophers and other intellectuals from France.

Figure 3-p. They turned their back on God's word and explained the world around them with "Mother Nature."

So we see, beginning (I use the word "beginning" with regard to our present study knowing that the roots of this conflict goes back much farther than this), with the mixture of Greek paganism introduced into Christian thinking by Thomas Aquinas, a tiny uneventful snowball would soon become a thunderous, destructive avalanche. As Immanual Kant,* an eighteenth century German philosopher, pointed out in his *What is Enlightenment?*:

> ...*The Enlightenment requires nothing but freedom—and the most innocent of all that may be called "freedom": freedom to make public use of one's reason in all matters...**Dare To Know!** (sapere aude) Have the courage to use your **own** understanding, is therefore the motto of the Enlightenment...* [168] (emphasis added)

Hence to Enlightenment thinkers, man was autonomous and his reason sovereign. The church, the Bible, and God were and no longer considered to be reliable sources for truth. [169] Sound familiar? Compare the following:

> *Where is the wise Man? Where is the scholar? Where is the philosopher of this age? Has not God made foolish the wisdom of this world?* **For since in the wisdom of God the world through its wisdom did not know Him, God was pleased through the foolishness of what was preached to save those who believe.** (I Corinthians 1:20-23 NIV)

After Renaissance influence was accumulated and was joined with the secularization of the Reformation, all of which was supported by the fallout of the Enlightenment, the stage was set for the coming blight of 19th century English scientism. The crowning work of Victorian England was Charles Darwin's (see Figure 3-q), famous book *The Origin of Species* (it really

---

*Gay said of Kant, "No one figure embodies the Enlightenment, but if any one could be singled out, it would be Immanual Kant." Peter Gay, The Enlightenment: A Comprehensive Anthology (New York: Simon and Schuster, 1973), p. 383. Also cited in Lindsell, New Paganism, p. 87.

shouldn't have been, but it is without a doubt the most prevailing product of this period). Today, after one hundred and thirty years of a Darwinian diet, the United States and the Western World are completely influenced by its many religious, scientific, educational and political ramifications.

Figure 3-q. Charles Darwin (1809-1882), did not invent the modern ideas of naturalistic evolution. He simply popularized an ancient notion about origins.

EVOLUTIONISM: OUR PRESENT WORLD VIEW

The tragic and final condition of this entire scenario has been the overthrow of God as the supreme Ruler in the affairs of man, and the subsequent ordination of man as "king." This present world view is founded on the materialism and naturalism popularized in ancient Greece, which of course, are the root causes of modern evolutionism. Modern evolutionism, marching under the banner of sound scientific knowledge, gives present-day atheism academic sanction. Dr. Lindsell unhesitatingly asserts that:

> *It would be amiss to overlook the great power of evolution as propounded by Charles Darwin in his Origin Of Species and by those who have followed closely in his footsteps. This theory of how things came into being and how humanoids have developed from lower forms of primate life and ultimately from the first cell has been a part of the **Enlightenment heritage that has destroyed the Judeo-Christian Weltanschauung [world view] in the West.** [170]*
> (emphasis added)

A careful examination of Darwin's work, *The Origin of Species by Means of Natural Selection*, will reveal that he developed his ideas a priori (by reason only), and that regardless of his claims, as I have already said, he never proved that one species arises from another species, and for that matter neither has anyone else. [171] Obviously, evolution is only at best a hypotheses (a mere conjecture), regarding the origin of life on earth, the age of the universe, etc., and nothing more. It is simply a belief system about the past.

Think about this—do you suppose A. I. Oparin, the Russian scientist (a modern supporter of organic evolution), really knew that the primordial atmosphere consisted of ammonia (NH_3), methane (CH_4), hydrogen (H_2), and water vapor (H_2O) ? [172] NO! He didn't know that at all. He simply guessed, a priori. His presupposition said that evolution was true and he was attempting to organize a feasible theory to explain it. Has his notions been thus proven? NO! Then why is this taught in public school science classes as scientific theory? Your guess is as good as mine—however, one fact is for sure, it is simply an ideological support system for the atheism, relativism, and the selfism in today's culture.

Moreover, how does Carl Sagan, probably the leading spokesman for evolutionary notions today, know that "The Cosmos is all that is or ever was or ever will be?" [173] He doesn't know! He simply reasons thusly from his belief system (or world view).

Figure 3-r. James Hutton (1726-1797), the father of uniformitarian geology, indicated that the present is the key to the past.

Furthermore, how did James Hutton (see Figure 3-r), the Scottish physician and scientist who popularized the notion of uniformitarianism, know that present processes affecting the structure of the earth have always been the same, and that to understand earth history all you need to do is to study present geological processes. [174] He didn't know this. This was simply based on his world view (and he was a deist, by the way).

The late well known journalist and philosopher, Malcolm Muggeridge, said in the Pascal Lectures at the University of Waterloo:

> *I myself am convinced that the theory of evolution, especially the extent to which it's been applied, will be one of the great jokes in the history books of the future. Posterity will marvel that so very flimsy and dubious a hypothesis could be accepted with the incredible credulity that it has."* [175]

The evidence is always weighed or interpreted through one's world view. Thus one person's world view gives one conclusion, while another world view leads to a different conclusion, and so on. There are as many interpretations and conclusions of any particular body of evidence as there are world views. Who's right?

One thing is for sure: in order for you to make the right conclusion about anything, you must know everything there is to know on all topics. This means you would have to be omniscient, and there is only One to whom that title can be given and that is—the Eternal God of Holy Scripture. Obviously, science will never know all there is to know about anything. Therefore, here's the dilemma. You will either form your knowledge base (which is both controlled by and also affects your world view), from the words of human scientists and philosophers (all of whom, obviously don't know all there is to know about anything, and who were not there in the beginning to observe the "big bang," or any of the rest of their Godless assumptions), or you will form your knowledge base from the science that is presented in God's Word. Ken Ham said it best:

> *The only way one could always be sure of arriving at the right conclusion about anything, including origins, depends upon one's knowing*

> *everything there is to know. Unless he knew that every bit of evidence was available, he could never really be sure that any of his conclusions were right. He would never know what further evidence there might be to discover and, therefore, whether this would change his conclusions. Neither could a person ever know if he had reached the point where he had all the evidence. This is a real problem for any human being—how can he ever be one hundred percent sure about anything? It is something of a dilemma, is it not?...However, starting with the irrefutable evidence of the Scriptures, we are told that in God the Father and His Christ "...are hidden all the treasures of wisdom and knowledge" (Colossians 2:3). There is no way any human mind can know all there is to know. But, we have someone who does...No human being, no scientist has all the evidence. That is why scientific theories change continuously. As scientists continue to learn new things, they change their conclusions.* [176]

Thus Ham asserts, to know anything for sure, or to form right conclusions about anything, we must begin with the Word of One who knows all things. I do not think I need to tell you "who" and/or "what" he was talking about. Of course he was pointing exclusively to the eternal Creator God and His Word, because God and His Word alone can provide a foundation worthy of my faith and obedience.

SUMMARY

I am deeply concerned that by covering so much history in so little space, I may have confused the reader regarding any or all of the people to whom I referred. You must remember, as Maitland said, history is a "seamless garment." In other words the church did not go to sleep one night and wake up the next morning to see the Hebrew-Christian influence going down the "tube." As Dr. Earle Cairns wrote, "There is a gradual transition from a view of life and human activity that characterized one era of history to a view that characterizes another." [177] This is why paradigm shifts are so infrequent and difficult. Therefore, when I say that this person said this, or that person wrote that, I am merely indicating that a transition is in place, and that depending on what they said or wrote with regard to the Bible and its message, can we interpret the direction of the transition. We must always remember that God is the author of History, and furthermore that nothing happens in the affairs of man that takes God by surprise. Oh, mystery of mysteries—the interconnection and accord between Sovereign grace and human volition?

Nevertheless, it can be openly observed in the Biblical narrative that God presents good and evil, righteousness and unrighteousness, and obedience or disobedience to all men. The Bible lucidly reports that [Jesus] **was that true Light, which lighteth every man that cometh into the world** (John 1:9). Accordingly, with little exception, man's opinion of the "Light," and the degree to which he follows the "Light," is controlled by his world view. Here is the peril—one's world view is received, by and large, from the socialization process that is common to the culture in which he is born (compare II Timothy 1:5, Proverbs 23:7, Luke 6:45, Colossians 2:8). If the values of a culture are antagonistic to Biblical principles, as they presently are in the West—especially in America, it is inordinately difficult for believers to maintain purity of thought and life. Furthermore, and extremely alarming, is the fact that the Biblical narrative reveals that God has once destroyed the world by water, and at other times rejected specific generations of whole nations—even Israel, when they became so corrupted in their world view that repentance and restoration was impossible. Another generation had to come on the scene that would follow God—but God always has had His Joshuas and His Calebs!

Knowing the foregoing to be true, I have attempted to show in this chapter many of the vital factors concerning the validity of knowledge and its relationship to our world view. It seems perfectly clear to me, that society builds within its cultural norms and values a safeguard that insulates its general world view from opposing ideas. This means that knowledge is both defined by and supportive of the prevailing world view in any society. This phenomenon is quite inconsequential to the Christian believer so long as their acceptance of human knowledge is limited to the simple cause/effect relationships that can be observed taking place in the physical world. However, in matters of total reality and first origins, it becomes vital that the believer unequivocally follows, and only follows, the inspired words of the Scripture. Do we, today? Alas, I think not!

There was a time when the prevailing world view in the West was Biblically Christian, and generally, total reality and first origins were seen and believed as it is presented in the Holy Bible (specifically the first eleven chapters of Genesis). Yet, all of that changed, and now you and I are completely bombarded on all fronts by secular, materialistic evolutionism. It influences our priorities, our relationships, our education, our government, even our churches. Where are the Joshuas and Calebs, today?

What can we do? Better yet, what must we do? We must return to the Bible for truth—we must search our beliefs and our behaviors carefully, and reject all ideas and demeanors that are not consistent with science (*knowledge*), according to Moses.

RESOURCE NOTES

PROLOGUE

1. A. E. Wilder-Smith, *The Creation of Life: A Cybernetic Approach To Evolution* (Wheaton, Illinois: Harold Shaw Publishers, 1970, 1974), pp. 13-14. Dr. Smith studied natural sciences at Oxford University and in 1941 received his Ph.D. in organic chemistry from Reading University. In 1964, he earned his second doctorate (Doctor of Science), from the University of Geneva, and during the same year he received his third doctorate at the E.T.M. in Zurich. From 1964 to 1970, Dr. Smith was Professor of Pharmacology at the Medical Center at the University of Illinois. He is also the author of many books and professional articles. Dr. Smith is a dedicated Christian and presently spends a lot of his time travelling around the world lecturing on creation science.

2. A. E. Wilder-Smith, *The Scientific Alternative to Neo-Darwinian Evolutionary Theory: Information Sources and Structures* (Costa Mesa, California: TWFT Publishers, 1987), p. ii.

3. Francis Brown, et al., *The New Hebrew and English Lexicon* (Lafayette, Indiana: Associated Publishers and Authors, Inc., 1978), p. 335.

4. Dewey Bertolini, *Youth Trends in the 21st Century*. A lecture given at the International Fellowship of Christian School Administrators sponsored by Association of Christian School International (ACSI, P.O. Box 4097, Whittier, California 90607, 1989). Mr. Bertolini is a professor at Master's College, an evangelical Christian, liberal arts college in California.

5. Ibid.

6. Ibid.

7. Charles Colson, *Kingdoms in Conflict* (Grand Rapids, Michigan: Zondervan Publishing House, 1987), p. 220. Charles Colson received his bachelor's degree from Brown University and his law degree from George Washington University. He served President Nixon as special advisor from 1969-1973. He is chairman of Prison Fellowship Ministries and has written several other best-selling publications.

8. Ernst Mayr, "The Nature of the Darwinian Revolution", *Science*, Vol. 176, June 2, 1972, p. 981.

9. James Moore, *Darwin: The Life of a Tormented Evolutionist* (New York: Warner, 1991), p. xxi.

10. Theodosius Dobzhansky, *Mankind Evolving: The Evolution of the Human Species* (New York: Bantam, 1970).

11. Colin Brown, *Philosophy and the Christian Faith* (Wheaton, Illinois: Tyndale, 1971), p. 147.

12. Newman Watts, *Why Be an Ape?: Observations on Evolution*. (London: Marshall, Morgan & Scott, Ltd., n.d.), p. 97.

13. Samuel Eliot Morison and Henry Steele Commager, *The Growth of the American Republic* (New York: Oxford University Press, 1942), p. 269. Professor Morison was the Jonathan Trumbull Professor of American History at Harvard University, and Professor Commager was Professor of History at Columbia University.

CHAPTER 1

WORLD VIEW: THE GOD THAT GOVERNS

14. William K. Purves and Gordon H. Orians, *Life: The Science of Biology* (Sunderland, Massachusetts: Sinauer Associates, Inc., 1987), p. 18. William Purves is from Harvey Mudd College, Claremont, California, and Gordon Orians is with

the University of Washington, Seattle. This volume is a popular textbook being used for freshman-sophomore biology classes at the college level.

15. Daniel D. Chiras, *Environmental Science: A Framework for Decision Making* (Menlo Park, California: Addison-Wesley Publishing Company, 1989), p. 28. Professor Chiras is with the University of Colorado at Denver. This book is a high school level science text and is adopted for use in the state of Oklahoma.

16. Ibid.

17. William Purvis and Gordon H. Orians, pp. 18-19.

18. Ibid, p. 28.

19. Ibid, p. 28.

20. Roger Lewin, *Bones of Contention* (New York: Simon and Schuster, 1987), p. 19. Roger Lewin is a professional paleoanthropologist and collaborated with Richard Leakey in the writing of the book, *Origins*. He has also authored other books and articles. He served as Science editor of *New Science*, and he works with the American Association for the Advancement of Science.

21. Harold Lindsell, *The New Paganism* (San Francisco: Harper & Row, Publishers, 1987), p. 45. Dr. Lindsell earned in Ph.D. in history from New York University. He is editor emeritus of *Christianity Today* and a member of the board at Wheaton College, as well as a professor at Simon Greenleaf School of Law. Furthermore, every serious Christian should also read his classic work: *Battle for the Bible*.

22. Francis A. Schaeffer, *Christian Manifesto* (Westchester, Illinois: Crossway Books, 1981), p. 31. Dr. Schaeffer was without a doubt one of the most influential Christian thinkers of this century. His twenty-two books, with more than three million copies in print, have been translated into twenty-five languages. His uncompromising style and grasp of historic Biblical Christianity gives his speaking and writing a prophetlike power.

23. Francis A. Schaeffer, pp. 31-32.

24. Terry Eastland, *"In Defense of Religious America"*, Commentary (June, 1981), p. 39. Cited in Schaeffer pp. 37-38.

25. Verna M. Hall, *The Christian History of the American Revolution* (San Francisco: Foundation for American Christian Education, 1976), p. 615. Cited in McDowell and Beliles, *Principles for the Reformation of the Nations*, Appendix. Also cited in David Barton, *The Myth of Separation*, p. 127. Originally, Noah Webster, *Holy Bible: Containing the Old and New Testament in Common Version* (New Haven, 1833), preface.

26. Lindsell, p. 45.

27. Will Durant, *Adventures In Genius* (New York: Simon and Schuster, 1931), p. 22. Durant said, "...if [Darwin] was right, men will have to date from 1859 the beginning of modern thought." Of course, 1859 is the date Darwin published his first edition of *Origin of Species*. Durant (1885-1981), was schooled as a boy in Catholic schools and completed his undergraduate work at St. Peter's College, Jersey City, and Columbia University. In 1909, he entered seminary at Seaton Hall College but left in 1911, and in 1913 he began his graduate studies at Columbia where he studied biology under the famous Dr. Thomas Hunt Morgan and philosophy under John Dewey. Does this tell you something about Durant's world view? He received his Ph.D. in philosophy in 1917. He became a prolific writer of history and philosophy, having authored many volumes.

28. Fran Sciacca, *Generation At Risk* (Minneapolis, Minnesota: World Wide Publications, 1990), p. 130. Sciacca is a graduate of Denver Seminary and has spoken on youth-related themes at family conferences and on Dr. James Dobson's Focus on the Family radio broadcast. He is also an instructor of one of the nation's largest Christian high schools in Colorado Springs and has authored several other books and studies.

29.   Harold Lindsell, p. 120.
30.   Francis A. Schaeffer, pp. 17-18.
31.   Michael Denton, *Evolution: A Theory in Crises* (Bethesda, Maryland: Adler & Adler Publishers, Inc., 1986), pp. 66-67. Dr. Denton is a medical doctor in Australia, as well as a research biochemist.
32.   Archibald Thomas Robertson, *Word Pictures In the New Testament* (Nashville, Tennessee: Broadman Press, 1932), Vol. 5, p. 433. Dr. Robertson was probably the most outstanding Greek scholar in the conservative Evangelical community of this century. He was professor of Greek New Testament at Southern Baptist Theological Seminary for nearly a half century. Among his many works is the voluminous and scholarly *A Grammar of the Greek New Testament in the Light of Historical Research*.
33.   Ralph Earle, *Word Meanings in the New Testament* (Grand Rapids, Michigan: Baker Book House, 1986), p. 429. Dr. Earle earned a Th.D. at Gordon Divinity School and did postdoctoral study at Harvard and Edinburg Universities. He was a pastor, as well as a distinguished Professor of the New Testament at the Nazarene Theological Seminary in Kansas City.
34.   William Edwyn Vine, *Expository Dictionary of Old and New Testament Words* (Iowa Falls, Iowa: World Bible Publishers, 1981), Vol. 1, p. 120. W. E. Vine (1873-1949), received an M.A. in Classics from London University. His most notable work, of the many he authored, is probably *An Expository Dictionary of New Testament Words*.
35.   Philip Appleman, p. 649.
36.   William Purves and Gordan Orians, p. 19.
37.   Herbert Wendt, *In Search of Adam* (Boston: Houghton Mifflin Company, 1955), illustration 12, p. 224. Herbert Wendt was born in Germany and considered by some to

be a highly regarded scholar of natural science and philosophy. His many works all have an evolutionary slant.
    38.   Francis A. Schaeffer, p. 18.

CHAPTER 2

MIXTURE: THE CURSE OF THE FALL

    39.   Michael Denton, *Evolution: A Theory in Crises* (Bethesda, Maryland: Adler & Adler Publishers, Inc., 1985), p. 358.
    40.   Rene Dubos, *"Humanistic Biology"*, American Scientist 53 (March, 1965): 6. Also cited in Henry M. Morris, *The Long War Against God*, pp. 21 & 146. Dr. Dubos was a French-American microbiologist who received his doctorate from Rutgers University. His work influenced Sir Alexander Fleming who is credited with the discovery of penicillin.
    41.   *Webster's Ninth New Collegiate Dictionary* (Springfield, Massachusetts: Merriam-Webster Inc., Publishers, 1987), p. 435.
    42.   John A. Garraty, *The American Nation: A History of the United States* (New York: Harper & Row, Publishers, Inc. 1966), p. 592. Garraty is a distinguished historian, writer, and Professor of History at Columbia University. Besides being a prolific writer, Garraty was a former president of the Society of American Historians, editor of the Dictionary of American Biography, a co-editor of the Encyclopedia of American Biography, and a member of the advisory board of American Heritage magazine.
    43.   Julian Huxley, "A New World Vision", *The Humanist 39* (March/April, 1979): 35-36. Also cited in Morris, *Long War*, p. 19. Huxley was the grandson of Thomas Huxley (Darwin's Bulldog), and a Professor of Zoology at Balliol College, Oxford, Rice Institute, and King's College, London. He was a

prolific author, as well as being one of the most influential evolutionists of the nineteenth century.

44. The open defection from the Biblical principle that explains the human personality and human interaction is seen in Dr. Ian Robertson's book, *Sociology*. Dr. Robertson is a popular sociological researcher and author. He received his doctorate in the sociology of education from Harvard. In his book he writes:

> *Alone among living creatures, human beings are fully self-aware—capable of inquiring and reflecting about themselves. Throughout history, our ancestors pondered human nature as it is revealed in the social life of our species. Why do human beings form families and why do they worship gods? Why is the way of life of one group so different from that of another? What makes some people break social rules while others obey them? Why are some people rich when others are poor? What makes one group go to war with another? What might a human being who had been raised in the company of other people be like? What holds societies together, and why do all societies change over time?*

Of course, the answer to these questions are all explained by the Word of God. However when the Bible is no longer considered scientific, as in our "scientific" age, one takes the following approach in finding these answers:

> *Until quite recently the answer to these and similar questions came from intuition, from speculation, and from the dead weight of myth, superstition and traditional "folk wisdom" handed down from the past. Only in the last century or so has a **new** method been applied to the study of human and social*

> *behaviors: **the method of science**, which provides answers drawn from facts collected by systematic research.* (emphasis added)

The above two quotes were taken from Ian Robertson, *Sociology* (New York: Worth Publishers, Inc., 1981), p. 3.

45. Modern psychology has also derived its approach and rationale from evolutionary theory. Dr. Morris writes:

> *There is probably no academic field of study and application more thoroughly saturated with evolutionary thinking than psychology and the other fields dealing with human behavior. Ever since Darwin—and especially since Freud—psychologists have assumed that man is merely an evolved animal and have evaluated his behavioral problems on an animalistic basis. Experiments with monkeys or other animals (even with insects), are used for guidance in dealing with human problems.*

This approach is wrong because man is not an "animal." He did not evolve from other life forms but was created in the image of God, with an eternal soul. Ironically, "psychology" means "study of the soul", but modern psychologists do not even believe in the soul (*Long War*, pp. 32-33).

46. American law and polity also bowed to Darwinism as Dr. John Eidsmoe has written:

> *The American legal community accepted Darwinism as quickly as every other element of society. As a result, many intellectual leaders in the late nineteenth and early twentieth century legal circles no longer felt comfortable with the Biblical or Blackstonian view that the civil law should reflect the law of God. As*

> *they rejected the Biblical view of law, a new legal philosophy was needed to fill the vacuum. That which arose is called legal positivism. Legal positivism, of course, is but one aspect of the total philosophy of positivism. It is said to have begun with Auguste Comte (1798-1857), who denied the existence of absolute, fixed, God-given truth. It could be said that Comte absolutely denied the existence of absolutes! Truth, he said, consists only in that which can be seen or heard or smelled or touched or felt—that which can be empirically verified by the scientific method. As society advances toward maturity, it casts off theological and metaphysical concepts and confines its interest to scientifically observable phenomena.*

John Eidsmoe, *The Christian Legal Advisor* (Grand Rapids, Michigan: Baker Book House, 1984), pp. 74-75.

47.   American educational policy and methodology also left Biblical precincts and rushed into the sinking sand of evolutionism. The man who championed this cause was John Dewey:

> *From the Darwinian theory Dewey drew important inferences. In early times when nature was explained in terms of divine design, philosophers considered change to be illusory and reality to lie in the eternal purposes of God. But the world described by Darwin was a place not merely of constant change but one in which chance played its part in the struggle for survival. The new science demanded a new philosophy, one that would forswear [reject]...inquiry after absolute origins and absolute finalities in order to*

> *explore specific values and the specific conditions that generate them.*
>
> *In the Darwinian theory Dewey also found his clue to the origin and nature of the human mind. The mind was not some mysterious substance different from the body; it was a "capacity" or an "ability" to cope with the environment which the human organism had acquired during its evolution. "Mind", said Dewey, "appears in experience as ability to respond to present stimuli on the basis of anticipation of future possible consequences, and with a view to controlling the kind of consequences that are to take place". From this it followed that the purpose of thinking was to decide what to do in specific situations. Ideas, in Dewey's simply phrase, were "plans of action". They were instruments for adjusting the organism to its environment.*

Nelson Manfred Blake, *A History of American Life and Thought* (New York: McGraw-Hill Book Company, 1972), p 441.

    48.   The word philosophy simply means a love of wisdom. No greater wisdom is possible than that can be received from the eternal Creator (Colossians 2:3; I Corinthians 1:18-25). Dr. Morris also points out that:

> *The fact is that, throughout history, intellectual leaders in every nation have yielded to this very temptation, placing human wisdom on a pedestal and rejecting or ignoring God's wisdom as inscripturated in the Bible. The result is philosophy, the "love of wisdom". This English word is derived from two Greek*

words, both used frequently in the New Testament and meaning, respectively, "love" and "wisdom". As such, it is regarded in the Bible as utterly wrong, to be completely rejected by Christian believers.

Actually the word itself [philosophy] is used only twice in any form in the Bible, but both these passages are very important and instructive. Colossians 2:8 contains the following warning: "Beware lest any man spoil you through philosophy and vain deceit, after the tradition of men, after the rudiments of the world, and not after Christ." (Colossians 2:8)

In this unique occurrence of "philosophy," believers are warned to beware of it! It is humanistic ("the tradition of men"), worldly, deceitful, and futile ("vain deceit"), rejecting the true wisdom in Jesus Christ.

Henry M. Morris, *Education For The Real World* (San Diego, California: Master Books, 1983), pp. 99-100. Dr. Morris, the father of the twentieth century revival of Biblical creationism, is president of the Institute for Creation Research of El Cajon, CA, and the author of more than 40 books. He received his Ph.D. from the University of Minnesota. He served 13 years as head of the Civil Engineering Department at the Virginia Polytechnic Institute and State University.

    49. Steve C. Dawson, *God's Providence in America's History* (Rancho Cordova, California: Steve C. Dawson, 1988), p. I:5. Also cited in David Barton, *The Myth of Separation*, pp. 25, 118, 158.

    50. William McDonald, ed., *Documentary Source Book of American History*, 1606-1889 (New York: MacMillan Company, 1909, p. 19. Also cited in Pat Robertson, *America's*

Dates With Destiny (Nashville, Tennessee: Nelson Publishers, 1986), p. 31.

51. Henry S. Commager, ed., *Documents of American History* (New York: Appleton Century-Crofts, Inc., 1948), p. 18. Also cited in Barton, p. 85.

52. Peter Marshall and David Manuel, *From Sea To Shining Sea* (Tarrytown, New York: Fleming H. Revell Company, 1986), p. 23. Also Democracy, Liberty, and Property: Readings in the American Political Tradition, Francis W. Coker, ed. (New York: MacMillan Company, 1942), pp. 18-19, and Barton, p. 85.

53. Verna M. Hall and Rosalie J. Slater, *The Bible and the Constitution of the United States of America* (San Francisco: The Foundation for American Christian Education, 1966), p. 15. Also cited in *Democracy, Liberty, and Property*, p. 20, and Barton, p. 85.

54. David Barton, *The Myth of Separation* (Aledo, Texas: Wall Builder Press, 1991), p. 86. Also cited in Commager, Documents of American History, p. 32. David Barton, an excellent Christian historian, is the president of WallBuilders, Inc., a Christian organization dedicated to the restoration of America's Biblical Christian foundation.

55. Ibid, p. 86. Also cited in Stephen K. McDowell and Mark A. Beliles, *America's Providential History*, p. 60; and J. Moss Ives, *The Ark and the Dove* (New York: Cooper Square Publishers, Inc., 1969), p. 119.

56. Ibid, p. 86. Also, Verna Hall, *The Christian History of the United States* (San Francisco: The Foundation for American Christian Education, 1966), p. 193. Taken from William Bradford, *Of Plymouth Plantation*, 1650, which has been translated in modern English by Harold Paget, *Bradford's History of the Plymouth Settlement*, 1608-1650 (San Antonio: Mantle Ministries, 1988), p. 21.

57. Ibid, p. 87. Also found in *North Carolina History*, Hugh Talmage Lefler, ed. (Chapel Hill: University of North Carolina Press, 1934, 1956), p. 16.

58. Ibid, p. 87. Also cited in Pat Robertson, *America's Dates With Destiny*, p. 32.

59. McDowell and Beliles, *America's Providential History* (Charlottesville, Virginia: Providence Press, 1988), p. 55. Also cited in Barton, p. 87.

60. Barton, p. 87.

61. *American Patriotism: Speeches, Letters, and Other Papers Which Illustrate the Foundation, the Development, the Preservation of the United States of America*, Selin H. Peabody, ed. (New York: American Book Exchange, 1880), p. 142. Also cited in Barton, p. 99.

62. B. F. Morris, *The Christian Life and Character of the Civil Institutions of the United States* (Philadelphia: George W. Childs, 1864), pp. 253-254. Also cited in Barton, p. 110.

63. John Jay, *The Correspondence and Public Papers of John Jay*, 1794-1826, Henry P. Johnston, ed. (New York: Burt Franklin, 1970), Vol. IV, p. 393, October 12, 1816. Also cited in Barton, p. 119.

64. Fran Sciacca, *Generation at Risk* (Minneapolis, Minnesota: World Wide Publications, 1990), p. 83.

65. Ibid, p. 83.

66. Ibid, p. 84.

67. James Davison Hunter, *Evangelicalism: The Coming Generation* (Chicago: The University of Chicago Press, 1987), p. 213. Professor Hunter teaches sociology at the University of Virginia and as authored and co-authored several other major works.

68. Ibid, p. 24.

69. Ibid, p. 24.

70. Tim LaHaye, *Faith Of Our Founding Fathers* (Brentwood, Tennessee: Wolgemuth & Hyatt, Publishers, Inc.), pp. 41-42. Dr. LaHaye quotes from Michael Farris, "The Real Meaning of the Declaration of Independence," *Concerned Women for American News*, Vol. 8 (July, 1986), pp. 3, 16:

> **The Declaration of the United States is our Charter.** It is the legal document that made us a nation like all the other nations of the world. It doesn't tell us how we are going to run our

country—that is what our Constitution does. In a corporation, the Charter is higher than the By-laws and the By-laws must be interpreted to be in agreement with the Charter. Therefore, the Constitution of the United States must be in agreement with the Declaration of the United States (more commonly known as the Declaration of Independence). The most important statement in our Declaration is that we want to operate under the laws of God.
(emphasis added)

Dr. LaHaye earned his Doctor of Ministry degree from Western Baptist Conservative Baptist Seminary. He is president of Family Life Seminar and chancellor of Christian Heritage College. He has also authored many books and publications.

71. Hunter, p. 39
72. Ibid, p. 65.
73. Ibid, p. 65.
74. Ibid, p. 65.
75. Sciacca, pp. 147-148.
76. Sciacca, p. 152.
77. Charles Colson, *Kingdoms In Conflict* (Grand Rapids, Michigan: Zondervan Publishing House, 1987), p. 214.
78. Sciacca p. 132.
79. Hunter, p. 68.
80. Sciacca, pp. 135-136.
81. Robert Frost. "The Road Not Taken", *Adventures in American Literature* (Orlando, Florida: Harcourt Brace Jovanovich, Publishers, 1989), p. 741.
82. Hunter, p. 68.
83. *Humanist Manifesto II*, Paul Kurtz, ed. (New York: Prometheus Books, 1973), p. vi.
84. Hilgard and Atkinson, *Introduction of Psychology*, Fourth Edition (Harcourt, Brace and World, 1967), p. 30.

85. Henry M. Morris, *The Long War Against God* (Grand Rapids, Michigan: Baker Book House, 1989), p. 32-33.

86. Daniel Goleman, *"Lost Paper Shows Freud's Effort to Link Analysis and Evolution"*, New York Times, February 10, 1987, p. 19. Cited in Morris, p. 33.

87. Morris, p. 33.

88. Jay E. Adams, *Competent to Counsel* (Grand Rapids, Michigan: Baker Book House, 1970), p. 70ff. Dr. Adams received his Ph.D. from the University of Missouri. He has pastored several churches, written many books, and is a frequent lecturer at ministerial and Bible conferences.

89. Sciacca, p. 134.

90. J. I. Packer, "Introductory Essay", *The Death of Death in the Death of Christ*, by John Owen (London: The Banner of Truth Trust, 1959), pp. 1-2.

91. D. Martin Lloyd-Jones, *Studies In The Sermon On The Mount* (Grand Rapids, Michigan: Wm. B. Eerdmans Publishing Co., 1971), Vol. I, P. 33. Dr. Lloyd-Jones was a practicing physician for several years assisting the famous Lord Horder. He left medicine in 1927 and entered the Christian ministry. In 1938 he moved to London to share the ministry of Westminster Chapel in Buckingham Gate with the renowned Dr. G. Campbell Morgan. He remained there until he retired in 1968.

92. Sciacca, p. 138.

93. George Gallup, Jr. and Jim Castelli, *The People's Religion: America's Faith in the 90's* (New York: MacMillan Publishing Company, 1989), p. 78.

94. Sciacca, p. 140.

95. Nelson E. Hinman, *An Answer To Humanistic Psychology* (Irvine, California: Harvest House Publishers, 1980), p. 27. Nelson Hinman is a Biblical counselor and pastor, and has done vast research into the pros and cons of the present counselling mania in the Christian community.

96. Sciacca, p. 141.

CHAPTER 3

WHAT IS REAL KNOWLEDGE

97. Henry M. Morris, *Education For The Real World* (San Diego, California: Master Books, 1983), p. 29ff.

98. Philip Appleman, *Darwin* (New York: W. W. Norton & Company, 1970), p. 649.

99. Gordon R. Taylor, *In The Beginning* (New York: Harper & Row, 1983), p. 199. Taylor's quote was used by the American Scientific Affiliation, Teaching Science in a Climate of Controversy (Ipswich, Massachusetts: American Scientific Affiliation, 1986), p. 29.

100. Douglas J. Futuyma, *Science on Trial: The Case For Evolution* (Pantheon Books, New York, 1982), p. 197.

101. William K. Purvis and Gordon H. Orians, *Life: The Science of Biology* (Sunderland, Massachusetts: Sinauer Associates, Inc., 1987), pp. 18-19.

102. Matthew 12:30, King James Version.

103. Francis A. Schaeffer, *The Christian Manifesto* (Westchester, Illinois: Crossway Books, 1982), p. 18.

104. Richard Hofstadter, *Social Darwinism in American Thought* (Boston: The Beacon Press, 1944, 1955), p. 88. Dr. Hofstadter received his Ph.D. from Columbia University. He wrote many award winning books on historical issues of America.

105. John C. Whitcomb and Henry M. Morris, *The Genesis Flood* (Grand Rapids, Michigan: Baker Book House, 1961), p. 214. Dr. John C. Whitcomb holds a Th.D. and is Professor of Old Testament at Grace Theological Seminary, Winona Lake, Indiana.

106. Schaeffer, p. 18.

107. Ibid, p. 28.

108. Arno Clemens Gaebelein, *Christianity or Religion* (New York: Publication Office, "Our Hope", 1927), pp. 97-98.

109. Henry M. Morris and Gary E. Parker, *What is Creation Science* (El Cajon, California: Master Books, 1982), p. 20. Dr. Gary Parker teaches biology at Clearwater Christian College in Clearwater, Florida. He has written many books on creation science and lectures around the world on related topics.

110. John N. Moore, *How To Teach Origins* (Milford, Michigan: Mott Media, Inc., 1983), pp. 56-57. Dr. Moore was Professor of Natural Science at Michigan State University until his retirement in 1982.

111. Ibid, p. 58.

112. Henry M. Morris, *The Long War Against God* (Grand Rapids, Michigan: Baker Book House, 1989), p. 156.

113. *The Fundamentals*, R. A. Torrey, et al., eds. (Grand Rapids, Michigan: Baker Book House, 1989), p. 156.

114. Wolfgang Smith, *Teilhardism and the New Religion* (Rockford, Illinois: Tan Books, 1988), p. 5. Cited in Morris, *The Long War Against God*, p. 161.

115. L. Harrison Matthews, F.R.S., "Introduction", *The Origin of Species by Charles Darwin* (London: J.M. Dent & Sons, Ltd., 1972), p. x, xi.

116. Errol White, C.B.S., F.R.S., "A Little on Lung-Fishes", *Proceedings of the Linnean Society*, Vol. 177, 1966, p. 8. Errol White was the president of the Linnean Society and this quote was taken from his annual presidential address.

117. Ken Ham, *"Science and the Christian World View"*, an address given at the Christian World View Conference, March 8, 1991, Hyatt Regency, Schaumburg, Illinois. Sponsored by Christian Liberty Academy, 502 W. Euclid Ave., Arlington Heights, IL 60004. Ken Ham holds a B. App. Sc. in environmental biology from Queenland Institute of Technology and a Dip. Ed. from the University of Queenland. He is president and founder of Creation Science Foundation of Australia. He has written many books and is a much sought after Christian science lecturer around the world.

118. Francis A. Schaeffer, *How Should We Then Live?* (Old Tappan, New Jersey: Fleming H. Revell Co., 1976), pp. 51-52. Also cited in Tim LaHaye, *The Battle For The Mind* (Old Tappan, New Jersey: Fleming H. Revell Company, 1980), p. 29.

119. Edward McNall Burns, *Western Civilizations: Their History and Their Culture* (New York: W. W. Norton & Company, Inc. Eighth Edition, 1973), pp. 113, 119. Burns was Professor of History at Rutgers University. He also authored several major works on American History, including *James Madison: Philosophy of the Constitution*.

120. Harold Lindsell, *The New Paganism* (San Francisco: Harper & Row, Publishers, 1987) p. 57. Dr. Lindsell indicated that "some of the precursors of the Enlightenment philosophies were identified with the Renaissance, which had in it elements supportive of the ideas of the later philosophies" (p. 57).

121. Hutton Webster, *Modern European Civilization* (Lexington, Massachusetts: Heath and Company, 1920), p. 577.

122. Otto Scott, *"Losing Ground in the Twentieth: The Reason for the Church's Decline"*. A lecture presented at the fourth Midwest Annual Christian Reconstruction Conference; sponsored by Christian Liberty Academy. Otto Scott is a former journalist and veteran newsman, as well as being an astute historian and author. He has written nine books, such as *James I: The Fool as King, Robespirerre: The Voice of Virtue*, etc.

123. Louis Trenchard More, *The Dogma of Evolution* (Princeton University Press, 1925), p. 67. Professor More, of the University of Cincinnati, gave the contents of this book as a series of lectures in January of 1925 at Princeton University. Cited in Morris, *Long War*, p. 211.

124. Alan Richardson, *The Bible in the Age of Science* (London: SCM Press, Ltd., 1961), pp. 9-10. Professor Alan Richardson taught Christian Theology at the University of Nottingham. In an editorial review in the periodical Theology it was said about Dr. Richardson that: *"Professor Alan Richardson is a theologian whose praise is (or deserves to*

be), in all the churches on account both of the books which he has written himself and of those which he has edited."

125. Donald B. DeYoung, *Astronomy and the Bible* (Grand Rapids Michigan: Baker Book House, 1990), p.15. Donald DeYoung is Professor of Physics and Astronomy at Grace College, Winona Lake, Indiana. Even though there are several statements in the Bible as "the rising of the Sun and the going down of the same" (Psalm 113); "the going forth of the sun" (Psalm 19:6), etc., it must be understood that these verses simply show "language of appearance" (Morris, *The Biblical Basis for Modern Science*, p. 164). This does not mean that the writers of the Bible supported a geocentric view of the earth any more than the modern meteorologist does when he talks about the time of "sunrise" and "sunset". These modern weathermen know full well that the sun rises only because of the rotation of the earth around its axis, however, they use these expressions every day of the week.

126. Richardson, p. 11.
127. Richardson, p. 14.
128. Ibid, p. 14.
129. Ibid, pp. 14-15.
130. Charles E. Hummel, *The Galileo Connection* (Downers Grove, Illinois: Inter-Varsity Press, 1986), p. 23. Charles E. Hummel holds advanced degrees in chemical engineering from Yale, and Biblical literature from Wheaton, and has served as president of Barrington College and is currently director of faculty ministries for Inter-Varsity Christian Fellowship.
131. Richardson, p. 17.
132. Ibid, p. 16. Also cited in Hummel, pp. 13ff.
133. Ibid, p. 18.
134. Otto Scott, lecture (see note 122).
135. Paul C. Vitz, *Censorship: Evidence of Bias in our Children's Textbooks* (Ann Arbor, Michigan: Servant Books, 1986), p. 77f. Paul C. Vitz is Professor of Psychology at New York University and the author of *Modern Art & Modern Science* and *Sigmund Freud's Christian Unconscious*.

136. Charles Krauthammer, *"Scopes Revisited",* Washington Post Magazine, October 19, 1986.

137. Jeremy Rifkin, *Algeny* (New York: Penguin Books, 1984), p. 112

138. J. C. Stobart, *The Glory*, fourth ed., R. J. Hooper (London: Sidwick and Jackson, 1964).

139. J. C. Stobart, *The Grandeur*, fourth ed., W. J. Maguinness and H. Scullard (New York: Frederick A. Praeger, Publishers, 1961).

140. Otto Scott, lecture (see note 122).

141. Henry M. Morris, *Men of Science: Men of God* (El Cajon, California: Master Books, 1988), p. 13.

142. Richardson, p. 20.

143. Morris, *Men of Science: Man of God*, p. 16.

144. Hummel, p. 272.

145. Ibid, pp. 273-274. Also cited in Emile Caillet, *Journey into Light* (Grand Rapids, Michigan: Zondervan Publishing House, 1968), pp. 95, 96.

146. Gerald G. Walsch, "Scholasticism," article written for *American Peoples Encyclopedia* (New York: Grolier, Inc., 1965), Vol. XVI, p. 377-378.

147. Rousas John Rushdoony, *The Institutes of Biblical Law* (The Presbyterian and Reformed Publishing Company, 1973), p. 384.

148. Earl E. Cairns, *Christianity Through the Centuries* (Grand Rapids, Michigan: Zondervan Publishing House, 1954), p. 284. Dr. Cairns earned both a Th.D. and a Ph.D. and taught History and Political Science at Wheaton College.

149. V.H.H. Green, *Renaissance and Reformation* (London: Edward Arnold Publishers, Ltd., 1952, 1962), p. 55. Professor Green was the Lightfoot Scholar in Ecclesiastical History at the University of Cambridge.

150. Burton F. Beers, *World History: Patterns of Civilization* (Englewood Cliffs, New Jersey: Prentice-Hall, Inc.

1984), p. 283. Burton Beers is a Professor of History at North Carolina State University.

151. T. Walker Wallbank, Arnold Schrier, Donna Maier, and Patricia Gutierrez-Smith, *History and Life: The World And Its People* (Glenview, Illinois: Scott, Foresman and Company, 1984), 358ff.

152. Morris, *The Long War Against God*, pp. 255 ff.

153. Burns, p. 132.

154. Ibid, p. 133.

155. Ibid, p. 133.

156. Ibid, p. 133.

157. Morris, p. 185.

158. Jonathan Miller and Borin Van Loon, *Darwin For Beginners* (New York: Pantheon Books, 1982), p. 25.

159. Loren C. Eiseley, *Darwin's Century*, p. 9-10. Also cited in Morris, *The Long War Against God*, p. 185-186.

160. Ian T. Taylor, *In The Mind Of Men: Darwin And The New World Order* (Toronto: TFE Publishing, 1987), p. 9. Taylor is a research metallurgist turned producer-writer for science documentaries that are broadcast on U.S. and Canadian television.

161. Roland H. Bainton, *The Reformation of the Sixteenth Century* (Boston: The Beacon Press, 1963), p. 128.

162. Earle E. Cairns, pp. 299-300.

163. Robert A. Baker, *A Summary of Christian History* (Nashville, Tennessee: Broadman Press, 1959), p. 154-155. Dr. Baker received his Th. D. from Southwestern Baptist Theological Seminary and his Ph.D. in church history from Yale University. Until his retirement in 1981, he taught church history at Southwestern.

164. Herbert Lockyer, *Ancient Portraits in Modern Frames* (Grand Rapids, Michigan: Baker Book House, 1975), p. 18. Dr. Lockyer has written an overwhelming host of books, as well as holding several pastorates in Scotland and England for 25 years. He also taught for Moody Bible Institute 10 years, after which he returned to England and took up his residence in

Bromley, Kent, where he lived and devoted most of his time to writing.

165. Lindsell, pp. 42-43.

166. George Park Fisher, *The Reformation* (New York: Charles Scribner's Sons, 1912), pp. 456-457.

167. Peter Gay, *The Enlightenment: The Rise of Modern Paganism* (New York: W.W. Norton & Company, 1966, 1977), p. 256. Peter Gay is a Professor of History at Yale University.

168. Peter Gay, *The Enlightenment: A Comprehensive Anthology* (New York: Simon and Schuster, 1973), pp. 384-389. Also cited in Lindsell, pp. 87-88.

169. Lindsell, p. 89. Quoting Kant, Lindsell wrote: "Thus spake Immanuel Kant: the human being is autonomous and reason supreme."

170. Ibid, p. 120.

171. Niles Eldredge, *Time Frames* (New York: Simon & Schuster, 1985), p. 33. Cited in Morris, p. 154. Niles Eldredge is Curator of Invertebrates at the American Museum of Natural History in New York. He is internationally known in the scientific community through his lectures and writings. He collaborated with Stephen J. Gould of Harvard in the formation of a mechanism for evolution known as "punctuated equilibrium."

172. Purvis and Orians, pp. 849-850.

173. Carl Sagan, *Cosmos* (New York: Random House, 1980), p. 4. Dr. Sagan is a Professor of Astronomy at Cornell University, as well as being a Pulitzer Prize-winning author. Sagan has been one of the most prominent evolutionists during the second half of the twentieth century.

174. M. Bowden, *The Rise of the Evolution Fraud* (San Diego, California: Creation-Life publishers, 1982), p. 19. In this regard, also note the comments of Dr. Gertrude Himmelfarb: "Uniformitarianism...imposed upon geologists too heavy a burden of abstract theory and speculation." Darwin and the Darwinian Revolution (New York: W. W. Norton & Company, Inc., 1962), p. 84.

175. Malcolm Muggeridge, *Pascal Lectures* (Ontario, Canada: University of Waterloo). Cited in Andrew Snelling, ed., *Quote Book* (Queensland, Australia: Creation Science Foundation, Ltd., 1990), p. 5. Dr. Snelling holds a Ph.D. in geology.

176. Ken Ham, *The Lie: Evolution* (El Cajon, California: Master Books, 1987), p. 19.

177. Cairns, p. 23.

BIBLIOGRAPHY

BOOKS

Adams, Jay E. *The Christian Counselor's Manual*. Grand Rapids, Michigan: Baker Book House, 1973, 1974.

Anderson, Irving H. and Dearborn, Walter F. *The Psychology of Teaching Reading*. New York: Ronald Press Company, 1952.

Appleman, Philip, ed. *Darwin*. New York: W. W. Norton & Company, Inc., 1970.

Asimov, Isaac *Asimov's Biographical Encyclopedia of Science and Technology*. Garden City, New York: Doubleday & Company, Inc., 1962, 1982.

Atkinson, Carroll and Maleska, Eugene T. *The Story of Education*. New York: Chilton Company, Book Div., 1962.

Augros, Robert and Stanciu, George. *The New Biology*. Boston: Shambhala Publications, 1987.

Bailey, Thomas A. *The American Pageant*. Lexington, Massachusetts: D. C. Heath and Company, 1956, 1975.

Bainton, Roland H. *The Reformation of the Sixteenth Century*. Boston: The Beacon Press, 1952, 1963.

Baker, Robert A. *A Summary of Christian History*. Nashville, Tennessee: Broadman Press, 1959.

Barna, George. *What Americans Believe*. Ventura, California: Regal Books, 1991.

Bartlett's Familiar Quotations: A Collecting of Passages Phrases and Proverbs Traced To Their Sources in Ancient and Modern Literature. Emily Morison Beck, ed. Boston: Little, Brown & Company, 1980.

Barton, David. *America: To Pray or Not To Pray*. Aledo, Texas: WallBuilder Press, 1989. 1991.

Barton, David. *The Myth of Separation*. Aledo, Texas: WallBuilder Press, 1989, 1991.

Beers, Burton, F. *World History: Patterns of Civilization*. Englewood Cliffs, New Jersey: Prentice-Hall, Inc., 1984.

Biological Sciences Curriculum Study (Written by forty-one writers).

Biological Science: Molecules to Man. (BSCS Blue Version), Boston: Houghton Mifflin Company, 1963.

Bird, Wendell R. *Harvard Journal of Law and Public Policy*. Wendell R. Bird, 1979.

Bird, Wendell R. *The Origin of Species Revisited*. (Two Volumes). New York: Philosophical Library, Inc., 1987, 1989.

Black, Eugene C. *Victorian Culture and Society*. New York: Walker and Company, 1974.

Blake, Nelson Manfred. *A History of American Life and Thought*. New York: McGraw-Hill Book Company, 1963, 1972.

Bliss, Richard B.; Parker, Gary E. and Gish, Duane T. *Fossils: Key To The Present*. San Diego, California: CLP Publishers, 1980.

Bowden, M. *The Rise of The Evolution Fraud*. San Diego, California: Creation Life Publishers, 1982.

Breese, Dave. *Seven Men Who Rule the World From the Grave*. Chicago: Moody Press, 1990.

Brown, Colin. *Philosophy and the Christian Faith*. Wheaton, Illinois: Tyndale, 1971, p. 147.

Brown, Francis, et. al. *The New Hebrew and English Lexicon*. Lafayette, Indiana: Associated Publishers and Authors, Inc., 1970

Burns, Edward McNall. *Western Civilizations: Their History and Their Culture*. New York: W. W. Norton & Company, Inc., Eighth Edition, 1973.

Burns, James MacGregor and Peltason, Jack Walter. *Government By The People: The Dynamics of American National Government*. Englewood Cliffs, New Jersey: Prentice-Hall, Inc., 1952, 1966.

Cairns, Earle E. *Christianity Through the Centuries: A History of the Christian Church*. Grand Rapids, Michigan: Zondervan Publishing House, 1954, 1967.

Cairns-Smith, A.G. *Seven Clues to the Origin of Life*. Cambridge: Cambridge University Press, 1985.

Cameron, James R. *Fredrick William Maitland and The History of English Law*. Norman: University of Oklahoma Press, 1961.

Chiras, Daniel D. *Environmental Science: A Framework for Decision Making*. Menlo Park, California: Addison-Wesley Publishing Company, 1989.

Clark, Robert E. D. *Darwin: Before and After*. Chicago: Moody Press, 1966, 1967.

Clark, Ronald W. *The Survival of Charles Darwin*. New York: Avon Books, 1984.

Clayton, John N. *The Source: Eternal Design or Infinite Accident*. South Bend, Indiana: John Clayton, 1976, 1983.

Coles, Robert and Genevie, Louis. "The Moral Life of America's Schoolchildren," *Teacher*. Vol. 1, Issue 6, March, 1990.

Colson, Charles. *Kingdoms in Conflict*. Grand Rapids, Michigan: Zondervan Publishing House, 1987.

Combs, Arthur W.; Blume, Robert A.; Newman, Arthur J.; and Wass, Hannelore L. *The Professional Education of Teachers: A Humanistic Approach to Teacher Preparation*. Boston: Allyn and Bacon, Inc., 1965, 1974.

Constable, George, ed. *This Fabulous Century* (1920-1930). Morristown, New Jersey: Silver Burdett Company, 1969, 1987.

Darwin, Charles. *The Origin of Species: or the Preservation of Favoured Races in the Struggle for Life*. London: Penguin Books, 1969 (first published by John Murray 1859).

Denton, Michael. *Evolution: A Theory in Crisis*. Bethesda, Maryland: Adler & Adler, Publishers., 1986.

DeYoung, Donald B. *Astronomy and the Bible*. Grand Rapids, Michigan: Baker Book House, 1990.

Dobzhansky, Theodosius; Ayala, Francisco J.; Stebbins, G. Ledyard and Valentine, James W. *Evolution*. San Francisco: W. H. Freeman and Company, 1977.

Dobzhansky, Theodosius. *Mankind Evolving: The Evolution of the Human Species*. New York: Bantam, 1970, p. 1.

Dolan, Edward F. Jr. *Adolf Hitler: A Portrait in Tyranny*. New York: Dodd, Mead & Company, 1981.

Earle, Ralph. *Word Meanings in the New Testament*. Grand Rapids, Michigan: Baker Book House, 1986.

Eidsmoe, John. *Christianity and the Constitution*. Grand Rapids, Michigan: Baker Book House, 1986.

Eidsmoe, John. *The Christian Legal Advisor*. Grand Rapids, Michigan: Baker Book House, 1984, 1987.

Eldredge, Niles. *Life Pulse: Episodes from the Story of the Fossil Record*. New York: Charles Scribner's Sons, 1912.

Fisher, George Park. *The Reformation*. New York: Charles Scribner's Sons, 1912.

Fleming, Thomas J. *The Golden Door*. Grosset & Dunlap, Inc., 1970.

Gaebelein, Arno Clemens. *Christianity or Religion*. New York: Publication Office "Our Hope," 1927.

Gallup, George, Jr., and Castelli, Jim. *The People's Religion*. New York: Macmillan Publishing Company, 1989.

Garraty, John A. *The American Nation*. New York: Harper & Row, Publishers, Inc., 1966.

Gaussen, L. *The Divine Inspiration of the Bible*. Grand Rapids, Michigan: Kregel Publications, 1971.

Gaustad, Edwin S. *Faith Of Our Fathers*. San Francisco: Harper & Row, Publishers, 1987.

Gay, Peter. *The Enlightenment: An Interpretation*. New York: W. W. Norton & Company, 1966.

Gilkey, Langdon. *Naming the Whirlwind: The Renewal Of God-Language*. Indianapolis: The Bobbs Merrill Company, Inc., 1969.

Gish, Duane T. *Evolution: The Challenge of the Fossil Record*. El Cajon, California: Master Books, 1985, 1986.

Green, V.H.H. *Renaissance and Reformation*. London: Edward Arnold (Publishers) OTD, 1952, 1965.

Hall, Verna M. and Slaten, Rosalie J. *The Bible and the Constitution of the United States of America*. San Francisco: The Foundation for American Christian Education, 1966.

Halley, Henry H. *Halley's Bible Handbook*. Chicago: Henry H. Halley, 1946.

Halstead, Beverly. Popper: "Good Philosophy, Bad Science", *New Science*. Vol. 87, No. 1210, July, 1980.

Ham, Ken. *The Lie: Evolution*. El Cajon, California: Master Books, 1973, 1984.

Ham, Ken and Taylor, Paul. *The Genesis Solution*. Grand Rapids, Michigan: Baker Book House, 1988.

Hamilton, Alexander. "Is a Bill of Rights Needed", *The Federalist Papers*. Andrew Hacker, ed. New York: Washington Square Press, Inc., 1964.

Harvard University (The Official Register of). Boston: Office of the University Publishers, Vol. XII, Number 7, August 20, 1991.

Himmelfarb, Gertrude. *Darwin and the Darwinian Revolution*. New York: W. W. Norton & Company, Inc., 1959, 1968.

Hinman, Nelson E. *An Answer To Humanistic Psychology*. Irvine, California: Harvest House Publishers, 1980.

Hodgins, Francis; Silverman, Kenneth; Stern, Milton R. and Hinojosa-Smith, Rolando R. *Adventures in American Literature*. Orlando: Harcourt Brace Jovanovich, Publishers, 1989.

Hofstadter, Richard. *Anti-Intellectualism in American Life*. New York: Alfred A. Knopf, 1963.

Hofstadter, Richard. *Social Darwinism in American Thought*. Boston: The Beacon Press, 1944, 1963.

Hoyle, Fred. *The Intelligent Universe*. New York: Holt, Rinehart and Winston, 1983.

Hogben, Lancelot. "Biology and Modern Racism," *Contemporary Jewish Record*. New York: The American Jewish Committee, Vol. IV, No. 1 February 1941.

Howard, Donald R. *To Save A Nation*. Lewisville, Texas: Accelerated Christian Education, Inc., 1976.

Hummel, Charles E. *The Galileo Connection*. Downers Grove, Illinois: Inter Varsity Press, 1986.

Hunter, George William. *New Civic Biology.* New York: American Book Company, 1914, 1926.

Hunter, James Davison. *Evangelicalism: The Coming Generation.* Chicago: The University of Chicago Press, 1987.

Johnson, Alvin W. and Yost, Frank H. *Separation of Church and State in the United States.* Minneapolis: University of Minnesota Press, 1934, 1948.

Johnson, William J. *George Washington: The Christian.* Milford, Michigan: Mott Media, 1976.

Karp, Walter. *Charles Darwin: And The Origin of Species.* New York: Harper & Row. 1968.

Kienel, Paul A., ed. *The Philosophy of Christian School Education.* Whittier, California: Association of Christian Schools International, 1978, 1980.

Krauthammer, Charles. "Scopes Revisited", *Washington Post Magazine.* October 19, 1986.

Kraus, Bertram S. *The Basis of Human Evolution.* New York: Harper & Row, Publishers, 1964.

Lindsell, Harold. *The New Paganism.* New York: Harper & Row, Publishers, 1987.

LaHaye, Tim. *The Battle for the Family.* Old Tappan, New Jersey: Fleming H. Revell Company, 1982.

LaHaye, Tim. *The Battle for the Mind.* Old Tappan, New Jersey: Fleming H. Revell Company, 1980.

LaHaye, Tim. *Faith of Our Founding Fathers*. Brentwood, Tennessee: Wolgemuth & Hyatt, Publishers, Inc., 1987, 1989.

Leakey, Richard E. and Lewin, Roger. *Origins*. New York: E. P. Dutton, 1977.

Lewin, Roger. *Bones of Contention*. New York: Simon and Schuster, 1987.

Lewin, Roger. *Human Evolution*. New York: W. H. Freeman and Company, 1984.

Lloyd-Jones, D. Martin. *Studies in the Sermon on the Mount*. Grand Rapids, Michigan: Wm. B. Eerdmans Publishing Company, 1971.

Lockyer, Herbert. *Ancient Portraits in Modern Frames*. Grand Rapids, Michigan: Baker Book House, Vol. II. 1975.

Lutz, Donald S. *The Origins of American Constitutionism*. Baton Rouge: Louisiana State University Press, 1988.

Lutz, Donald S. "The Relative Influence of European Writers on Late Eighteenth-Century American Political Thought", *The American Political Science Review*. Washington, D.C., Vol. 78, No. 1, March, 1984.

Marshall, Peter and Manuel, David. *The Light and the Glory*. Old Tappan, New Jersey: Fleming H. Revell Company, 1977.

Marshall, Peter and Manuel, David. *From Sea to Shining Sea*. Tarrytown, New York: Fleming H. Revell Company, 1986.

Matthews, L. Harrison. "Introduction", *Origin of Species*. By Charles Darwin. London: J. M. Dent & Sons LTD, 1971.

May, Arthur J. *The Story of Our Heritage*. New York: Charles Scribner's Sons, 1956, 1964.

Mayr, Ernst. "The Nature of the Darwinian Revolution", *Science*. Vol. 176, June 2, 1982, p. 981.

McCarthy, Martha M. *A Delicate Balance: Church, State, and the Schools*. Bloomington, Indiana: A Publication of the Phi Delta Kappan Educational Foundation, 1983.

Millard, Catherine. *The Rewriting of America's History*. Camp Hill, Pennsylvania: Horizon House Publishers, 1991.

Miller, Jonathan and Van Loon, Borin. *Darwin for Beginners*. New York: Pantheon Books, 1982.

Minton, Arthur J. and Shipka, Thomas A. *Philosophy: Paradox and Discovery*. New York: McGraw-Hill Publishing Company, 1976, 1990.

Moore, James. *Darwin: The Life of a Tormented Evolutionist*. New York: Warner, 1991, xxi.

Moore, John N. *How To Teach Origins (Without ACLU Interference)*. Milford, Michigan: Mott Media, Inc., 1983.

Morison, Samuel Eliot and Commanger, Henry Steel. *The Growth of the American Republic*. New York: Oxford University Press, 1930, 1946.

Morris, Desmond. *The Naked Ape*. New York: McGraw-Hill Book Company, 1967.

Morris, Henry M. *Education for the Real World*. San Diego, California: Master Books, 1977.

Morris, Henry M. *Men of Science Men of God*. El Cajon, California: Master Books, 1982, 1988.

Morris, Henry M. *Scientific Creationism*. El Cajon, California: Master Books, 1974, 1991.

Morris, Henry M. *The Biblical Basis for Modern Science*. Grand Rapids, Michigan: Baker Book House, 1984.

Morris, Henry M. *The Bible Has The Answer*. Grand Rapids, Michigan: Baker Book House, 1971, 1986.

Morris, Henry M. *The Genesis Record*. Grand Rapids, Michigan: Baker Book House, 1977, 1986.

Morris, Henry M. *The Long War Against God*. Grand Rapids, Michigan: Baker Book House, 1989, 1990.

Morris, Henry M. and Parker, Gary E. *What is Creation Science*. El Cajon, California: Master Books, 1982, 1987.

Nelkin, Dorothy. *The Creation Controversy: Science or Scripture in the Schools*. New York: W. W. Norton & Company, 1982.

Newton, David E. *U.S. and Soviet Space Programs*. New York: Franklin Watts, 1988.

North, Gary. *The Dominion Covenant: Genesis*. Tyler, Texas: The Institute for Christian Economics, 1982.

Norton, Mary Beth; Katzman, David M.; Escott, Paul D.; Chudacoff, Howard P.; Patterson, Thomas G. and Tutle, William M. *A People and a Nation*. Boston: Houghton Mifflin Company, 1986.

Osborn, Henry Fairfield. "The Evolution of Human Races", *Natural History*. January/February, 1926.

Packer, J. I. "Introductory Essay", *The Death of Death in the Death of Christ* (By John Owen). London: The Banner of Truth Trust, 1959.

Persons, Stow. *Evolutionary Thought in America*. Yale University Press, 1950, 1968.

Postman, Neil. *Amusing Ourselves to Death*. New York: Viking Penguin, Inc., 1985.

Purves, William K. and Orians, Gordon H. *Life: The Science of Biology*. Sunderland, Massachusetts; Sinauer Associates Inc., 1987.

Quint, Howard H.; Cantor, Milton and Albertson, Dean. *Main Problems in American History*. Chicago: The Dorsey Press, 1964, 1988.

Reader, John. *The Rise of Life: The First 3.5 Billion Years*. New York: Alfred A. Knopf, Inc., 1986.

Richard, Alan. *The Bible in the Age of Science*. London: SCM Press LTD, 1961.

Rifkin, Jeremy. *Algeny*. New York: Penguin Books, 1984.

Robertson, Ian. *Sociology*. New York: Worth Publishers, Inc., 1977, 1981.

Robertson, Pat. *America's Dates with Destiny*. Nashville: Thomas Nelson Publishers, 1986.

Ruse, Michael. *The Darwinian Revolution*. Chicago: The University of Chicago Press, 1979.

Rushdoony, Rousas John. *The Institutes of Biblical Law*. The Presbyterian and Reformed Publishing Company, 1973, 1978.

Rusk, Roger. *The Other End of the World*. Knoxville, Tennessee: Plantation House, Inc., 1988.

Ryrie, Charles C. *Basic Theology*. Wheaton, Illinois: Victor Books, 1987.

Sagan, Carl. *Cosmos*. New York: Random House, 1980.

Schaeffer, Francis A. *A Christian Manifesto*. Westchester, Illinois: Crossway Books, 1984.

Schaeffer, Francis A. *How Should We Then Live?* Old Tappan, New Jersey: Fleming H. Revell Company, 1976.

Schechter, Stephen L., ed. *Roots of the Republic*. Madison, Wisconsin: Madison House Publisher, Inc., 1990.

Sciacca, Fran. *Generation at Risk*. Minneapolis, Minnesota: World Wide Publications, 1990.

Snelling, Andrew. *Quote Book*. Queensland, Australia: Creation Science Foundation LTD, 1990.

Stern, David H. (translator). *Jewish New Testament*. Clarksville, Maryland: Jewish New Testament Publications, 1989.

Stobart, J.C. *The Glory*. London: Sidwick and Jackson, 1964.

Stobart, J.C. *The Grandeur*. New York: Frederick A. Praeger. 1961.

Sunderland, Luther D. *Darwin's Enigma*. El Cajon, California: Master Books, 1984.

Taylor, Gordon Rattray. *The Great Evolution Mystery*. New York: Harper & Row, Publishers, 1983.

Taylor, Ian T. *In The Minds of Men: Darwin and the New World Order*. Toronto: TFE Publishing, 1984, 1987.

Thaxton, Charles B.; Bradley, Walter L. and Olsen, Roger L. *The Mystery of Life's Origin: Reassessing Current Theories*. New York: Philosophical Library.

Thorndike, Edward L. *Animal Intelligence*. New York: The Macmillan Company, 1898.

Tiner, John Hudson. *When Science Fails*. Grand Rapids, Michigan: Baker Book House, 1974.

Torry, R. A.; Dixon, A. C., et al., eds. *The Fundamentals*. Grand Rapids, Michigan: Baker Book House, 1972.

Trueblood, Elton D. *Philosophy of Religion*. Grand Rapids, Michigan: Baker Book House, 1957, 1982.

Vine. W. E. *Vine's Expository Dictionary of Old and New Testament Words*. Iowa Falls: Iowa: World Bible Publishers, 1981.

Vitz, Paul C. *Censorship: Evidence of Bias in Our Children's Textbooks*. Ann Arbor, Michigan: Servant Books, 1986.

Wallbank, T. Walker; Schrier, Arnold; Maier, Donna and Gutierrez-Smith, Patricia. *History and Life: The World and its People*. Glenview, Illinois: Scott, Foresman and Company, 1984.

Watts, Newman. *Why Be An Ape?: Observations On Evolutionism*. London: Marshall, Morgan & Scott, Ltd., n.d., p. 97.

Webster, Noah. *American Dictionary of the English Language*. 1828. Reprinted San Francisco: Foundation of for American Christian Education, 1967.

Webster's Biographical Dictionary. Springfield, Massachusetts: G. & C. Merriam Co., Publishers, 1943, 1962.

Whitcomb, John C. and Morris, Henry M. *The Genesis Flood*. Grand Rapids, Michigan: Baker Book House, 1961.

White, Errol. "A Little on Lung-fishes", *Proceedings of the Linnean Society*. Vol. 177, 1966.

Whitehead, John W. *The Second American Revolution*. Elgin, Illinois: David C. Cook Publishing Company, 1982.

Wilder-Smith, A. E. *The Creation of Life: A Cybernetic Approach to Evolution*. Wheaton, Illinois: Harold Shaw Publishers, 1970, 1974.

Wilder-Smith, A. E. *The Scientific Alternative to Neo-Darwinian Evolutionary Theory: Information Sources and Structures*. Costa Mesa, California: TWFT Publishers, 1987.

Woodward, Kenneth L. "How the Bible Made America", *Newsweek*. December, 17, 1982.

Zirkle, Conway. *Evolution, Marxian Biology, and the Social Scene*. Philadelphia: University of Pennsylvania Press, 1959.

ENCYCLOPEDIAS AND SETS

American Peoples Encyclopedia. New York: Grolier Incorporated, 1965.

American Heritage Illustrated History of the United States. Englewood, Cliffs, New Jersey: Silver Burdett Press, Inc., 1989.

Annals of America, The. Chicago: Encyclopedia Britannica, Inc., 1976.

Cambridge Encyclopedia, The. London, Cambridge University Press, 1990.

Encyclopedia Britannica. Chicago: William Benton, Publisher, 1970.

Harper Encyclopedia of Science, The. James R. Newman, ed. New York: Harper & Row, Publishers, 1967.

International Standard Bible Encyclopedia, The. James Orr, ed. Grand Rapids, Michigan: Wm. B. Eerdman Publishing Co., 1939.

McGraw-Hill Encyclopedia of Science and Technology. New York: McGraw-Hill Book Company, 1977.

Old Testament Commentaries. By Keil and Delitzsch. Grand Rapids, Michigan: Associated Publishers and Authors, Inc.

Oxford Companion to American History, The. New York: Oxford University Press, 1966.

Religious Encyclopedia or Dictionary of Biblical, Historical, Doctrinal, and Practical Theology. Philip Schaff, ed. Toronato: Funk & Wagnalls Company, 1891.

Treasury of Religious Thought. H. D. M. Spence, Joseph S. Exell, and Charles Neil, eds. London: R.D. Dickinson, 1889.

Word Pictures in the New Testament. by A. T. Robertson. Nashville, Tennessee: Broadman Press, 1932.

World Book Encyclopedia, The. Chicago: World Book, Inc., 1985.

APPENDIX A

Bible-Believing Scientists of the Past
Scientific Disciplines Established by Bible-believing Scientists

Discipline	Scientist
Antiseptic Surgery	Joseph Lister (1827-1912)
Bacteriology	Louis Pasteur (1822-1895)
Calculus	Isaac Newton (1642-1727)
Celestial Mechanics	Johann Kepler (1571-1630)
Chemistry	Robert Boyle (1627-1691)
Comparative Anatomy	Georges Cuvier (1769-1832)
Computer Science	Charles Babbage (1792-1871)
Dimensional Analysis	Lord Rayleigh (1842-1919)
Dynamics	Isaac Newton (1642-1727)
Electrodynamics	James Clerk Maxwell (1831-1879)
Electromagnetics	Michael Faraday (1791-1867)
Electronics	Ambrose Fleming (1849-1945)
Energetics	Lord Kelvin (1824-1907)
Entomology of Living Insects	Henri Fabre (1823-1915)
Field Theory	Michael Faraday (1791-1867)
Fluid Mechanics	George Stokes (1819-1903)
Galactic Astronomy	William Herschel (1738-1822)
Gas Dynamics	Robert Boyle (1627-1691)
Genetics	Gregor Mendel (1822-1884)
Glacial Geology	Louis Agassiz (1807-1873)
Gynecology	James Simpson (1811-1870)
Hydraulics	Leonard da Vinci (1452-1519)
Hydrography	Matthew Maury (1806-1873)
Hydrostatics	Blaise Pascal (1623-1662)
Ichthyology	Louis Agassiz (1807-1873)
Isotopic Chemistry	William Ramsay (1852-1916)
Model Analysis	Lord Rayleigh (1842-1919)

APPENDIX A

Discipline	Scientist
Natural History	John Ray (1627-1705)
Non-Euclidean Geometry	Bernhard Riemann (1826-1866)
Oceanography	Matthew Maury (1806-1873)
Optical Mineralogy	David Brewster (1781-1868)
Paleontology	John Woodward (1665-1728)
Pathology	Rudolph Virchow (1821-1902)
Physical Astronomy	Johann Kepler (1571-1630)
Reversible Thermodynamics	James Joule (1818-1889)
Statistical Thermodynamics	James Clerk Maxwell (1831-1879)
Stratigraphy	Nicholas Steno (1631-1686)
Systematic Biology	Carolus Linnaeus (1707-1778)
Thermodynamics	Lord Kelvin (1824-1907)
Thermokinetics	Humphrey Davy (1778-1829)
Vertebrate Paleontology	Georges Cuvier (1769-1832)

Notable Inventions, Discoveries, or Developments by Bible-believing Scientists

Contribution	Scientists
Absolute Temperature Scale	Lord Kelvin (1824-1907)
Actuarial Tables	Charles Babbage (1792-1871)
Barometer	Blaise Pascal (1623-1662)
Biogenesis Law	Louis Pasteur (1822-1895)
Calculating Machine	Charles Babbage (1792-1871)
Chloroform	James Simpson (1811-1870)
Classification System	Carolus Linnaeus (1707-1778)
Double Stars	William Herschel (1738-1822)
Electric Generator	Michael Faraday (1791-1867)
Electric Motor	Joseph Henry (1797-1878)

Contribution	Scientists
Ephemeris Tables	Johann Kepler (1571-1630)
Fermentation Control	Louis Pasteur (1822-1895)
Galvanometer	Joseph Henry (1797-1878)
Global Star Catalog	John Herschel (1792-1871)
Inert Gases	William Ramsay (1852-1916)
Kaleidoscope	David Brewster (1781-1868)
Law of Gravity	Isaac Newton (1642-1727)
Mine Safety Lamp	Humphrey Davy (1778-1829)
Pasteurization	Louis Pasteur (1822-1895)
Reflecting Telescope	Isaac Newton (1642-1727)
Scientific Method	Francis Bacon (1561-1626)
Self-induction	Joseph Henry (1797-1878)
Telegraph	Samuel F. B. Morse (1791-1872)
Thermionic Valve	Ambrose Fleming (1849-1945)
Trans-Atlantic Cable	Lord Kelvin (1824-1907)
Vaccination and Immunization	Louis Pasteur (1822-1895)

The foregoing information first appeared in: Henry M. Morris, *The Biblical Basis for Modern Science* (Grand Rapids, Michigan: Baker Book House, 1984), pp. 463-465. Used with permission.

APPENDIX B

NECESSITY FOR DESIGN
LETTER FROM WERNHER VON BRAUN

On September 14, 1972 the following letter was written by Dr. Wernher von Braun, of NASA (father of our space program), to the California State Board of Education:

Dear Mr. Grose:

In response to your inquiry about my personal views concerning the "Case for DESIGN" as a viable scientific theory for the origin of the universe, life and man, I am pleased to make the following observations.

For me, the idea of creation is not conceivable without invoking the necessity of design. One cannot be exposed to the law and order of the universe without concluding that there must be design and purpose behind it all. In the world around us, we can behold the obvious manifestations of an ordered, structured plan or design. We can see the will of the species to live and propagate. And we are humbled by the powerful forces at work on a galactic scale, and the purposeful orderliness of nature that endows a tiny and ungainly seed with the ability to develop into a beautiful flower. The better we understand the intricacies of the universe and all it harbors, the more reason we have found to marvel at the inherent design upon which it is based.

While the admission of a design for the universe ultimately raises the question of a Designer (a subject outside of science), the scientific method does not allow us to exclude data which lead to the conclusion that the universe, life and man are based on design. To be forced to believe only one conclusion—that everything in the universe happened by chance—would violate the very objectivity of science itself. Certainly there are those who argue that the universe evolved out of a random process, but what random process could produce the brain of a man or the system of the human eye?

Some people say that science has been unable to prove the existence of a Designer. They admit that many of the miracles in the world around us are hard to understand, and they do not deny that the universe, as modern science sees it, is indeed a far more wondrous thing than the creation medieval man could perceive. But they still maintain that since science has provided us with so many answers the day will soon arrive when we will be able to understand even the creation of the fundamental laws of nature without a Divine Intent. They challenge science to prove the existence of God. But must we really light a candle to see the sun?

Many men who are intelligent and of good faith say they cannot visualize a Designer. Well, can a physicist visualize an electron? The electron is materially inconceivable and yet, it is so perfectly known through its effects that we use it to illuminate our cities, guide our airlines through the night skies and take the most accurate measurements. What strange rationale makes some physicists accept the inconceivable electrons as real while refusing to accept the reality of a Designer on the ground that they cannot conceive Him? I am afraid that, although they really do not understand the electron either, they are ready to accept it because they managed to produce a rather clumsy mechanical model of it borrowed from rather limited experience in other fields, but they would not know how to begin building a model of God.

I have discussed the aspect of a Designer at some length because it might be that the primary resistance to acknowledging the "Case for Design" as a viable scientific alternative to the current "Case for Chance" lies in the inconceivability, in some scientists' minds, of a Designer. The inconceivability of some ultimate issue (which will always lie outside scientific resolution), should not be allowed to rule out any theory that explains the interrelationship of observed data and is useful for prediction.

We in NASA were often asked what the real reason was for the amazing string of successes we had with our Apollo flights to the Moon. I think the only honest answer we could give was that we tried to never overlook anything. It is in that same sense of scientific honesty that I endorse the presentation of alternative theories for the origin of the universe, life and man in the science classroom. It would be an error to overlook the possibility that the universe was planned rather than happened by chance.

With kindest regards.

Sincerely,
Wernher von Braun

This letter appeared in the book written by Edward F. Blick, *Special Creation vs. Evolution* (Oklahoma City, OK: Southwest Radio Church, 1988), pp. 29-31. Used with permission.

APPENDIX C

SOURCES OF CREATION MATERIALS

U.S.A.

Bible-Science Association
2911 East 42nd Street
Minneapolis, MN 55406

Creation Research Society
2717 Cranbrook Road
Ann Arbor, MI 48104

Creation Science Association
18346 Beverly Road
Birmingham, MI 48009

Creation Science Association
2825 Riva Ridge Circle
Cottage Grove, WI 53527

Creation Science Ministries
P.O. Box 6330
Florence, KY 41022

Creation-Science Research
   Center
P.O. Box 23195
San Diego, CA 92123

Creation Social Science &
   Humanities Society
1429 North Holyoke
Wichita, KS 67208

Creation Truth Foundation, Inc.
P.O. Box 1435
Noble, OK 73068
800-554-9049

Geoscience Research
   Institute
Andrews University
Berrien Springs, MI 49104

Center for Scientific Creation
1319 Brush Hill Circle
Naperville, IL 60540

Institution for Creation
   Research
P.O. Box 2667
El Cajon, CA 92021-0667

Lutheran Science Institute
8830 West Bluemound Road
Milwaukee, WI 53226
(Membership restricted to Wisc.
Ev. Lutherans)

Maxwell Society of
Shoreland Lutheran High School
5043 20th Avenue
Kenosha, WI 53140

Missouri Association for
   Creation
2111 Princeton
St. Louis, MO 63117

Origins
Geoscience Research Institute
Loma Linda University
Loma, Linda, CA 92350

APPENDIX C

Pittsburgh Creation Society
208 S. Magnolia Drive
Glenshaw, PA 15116

Students for Origins
　Research
P.O. Box 203
Goleta, CA 93116

OVERSEAS

Biblical Creation Society
51 Cloan Crescent
Bishopbriggs
Glasgow, Scotland G64 2HN

Dr. David Lackman
North American Agent
316 Hamel Avenue
North Hills, PA 19038

Creation Science Assoc.
　of Australia
P.O. Box 302
Sunnybank, Queensland
Australia 4109

Creation Scientist Forum of
　India
Chalukunnu
Kottayam
Kerala 686001

A. Radcliffe-Smith, Hon. Sec.
Evolution Protest Movement
13 Argyle Avenue
Hounslow, Middlesex
England, TW3 2LE

Forening for Biblisk
　Skapelesetro
Box 50
424 21 Angered
Sweden

Newton Scientific Association
2 Westoe Road
Edmonton
London, England N9 OSH

CANADA

Creation Science Association
　of Canada
P.O. Box 34006
Vancouver, B.C. V6J 4M1

Creation Science Association
　of Alberta
P.O. Box 9075, Station "E"
Edmonton, Alta, T5P 4K1

Creation Science Association
　of Saskatchewan
Box 1821
Prince Albert, Sask, S6V 6J9

Creation Science Association
　of Ontario
P.O. Box 821, Station "A"
Scarborough, Ont. M1K 5C8

International Christian Crusade
205 Younge Street, Room 31
Toronto, Ont. M5B 1N2

North American Creation
　Movement
P.O. Box 5083, Station "B"
Victoria, B.C. V8R 6N3

PUBLISHERS

Baker Book House
P.O. Box 6287
Grand Rapids, MI 49506

Concordia Publishing House
3558 South Jefferson
St. Louis, MO 63118

Creation-Life Publishers, Inc.
Box 15666
San Diego, CA 92115

Creation Truth Publications
P.O. Box 1435
Noble, OK 73068
800-554-9049

Mott Media
1000 E. Huron
Milford, MI 48042

Creation Truth Publications
P.O. Box 1435
Noble, OK 73068
800-554-9049

Crossroads (Ian Taylor)
100 Huntley Street
Toronto, Ontario
Canada, M4Y 2L1

AUDIO-VISUAL SUPPLIERS

Eden Films
North Eden Road
Elmwood, IL 61529

CLP Video
P.O. Box 15666
San Diego, CA 92115

Creation Filmstrip
Center
Rt. 1
Haviland, KS 67059

INDEX

- A -

A priori: 115, 148
ACLU: See: American Civil Liberties Union
Adam: 29-31, 103
Agassiz, Louis: xli, 95,
Age of Reason: 90, 106, 144
AIDS: 76
American Bible Society: 51
American Civil Liberties Union: xxxiii
American Humanist Association: 65
Anaximander: 131
Anaximenes: 131
Anthropology: iv, 134
Aquinas, Thomas: v, 102, 113, 127, 145
Aristotle: v, 82, 104, 109, 111-116, 127, 131, 133-135
Asbury, Francis: 57
Autonomous: 41, 77, 146
Autonomy: 53, 76

- B -

Baby Boomer: xvii
Bainton, Roland H.: 135
Baker, Robert A.: 137
Baldwin, James: 57
Baltimore, Lord: 46
Baptist: xi, xxvii
Barnes, Thomas G.: xiii
Barton, David: xi, 48, 50
Beatitudes: 72, 73
Bertolini, Dewey: xxviii-xxx
Big Bang: 150
Blick, Edward F.: x, xiii
Bloom, Allen: 58
Bradford, William: 47
Brahe, Tycho: 96
Brown, Colin: xxxvii
Brown, Francis: xxv
Browning, Robert: 76
Bunyan, John: 54
Burns, Edward N.: 104
Butler, Larry: xiii

- C -

Cairns, Earle E.: 129, 136, 152
Calvin, John: 139
Capitalism: 39
Carnegie, Andrew: 39
Castelli, Jim: 75
Catholic: 104, 127, 137, 142
Chain of Being: 131, 134
Channing, William E.: 40
Christian Association of Psychological Studies: 64
Colson, Charles: xxxiii
Competition: 39
Comte, Auguste: 40
Congress: 8

Constitution: 46, 47, 55
Constitutional Convention 50
Copernicus, Nicolaus: 111, 115
Cosmology: 113, 115, 116
Cosmos: 15, 20, 35, 109, 149
Crabb, Larry: 61
Creation Truth Foundation, Inc.: 11
Curriculum: xxiii, xxvi, xxix, 43

- D -

d'Alembert, Jean: 144
Dark Ages: 105, 129
Darlington, R. J.: 20
Darwin, Charles: iii-v, xiv, xxx, xxxv-xxxviii, xli, xlii, xliv, 10, 11, 13, 15, 18, 34, 36, 38-41, 55, 66, 92, 98, 100, 106, 108, 133-135, 146, 148
Day-Age Theory: 36, 90
Declaration of Independence: 7, 55
Deism: 40, 135, 142
Democritus: 132
Denton, Michael: 34
Descent of Man: 99
Diderot, Denis: 144
Dobson, James: 61
Dobzhansky, Theodosius: xxxvi
Dubos, Rene: 35

- E -

Earle, Ralph: 16, 33, 95, 108
Eastland, Terry: 8
Eiseley, Loren: 134
Emerson, Ralph Waldo: 40
Enlightenment: xxi, xxxviii, 10-13, 99, 105, 106, 120, 143-146, 148
Epicurean: 109, 110
Evangelical: xv, xviii, xxxi, xlv, 13, 52, 54, 56, 60, 64, 65, 68, 73, 74, 76, 77
Evangelical Academy Project: 54
Existentialism: 39, 40

- F -

Fisher, George P.: 141
Founding Fathers: 7, 8, 44, 49, 53
Freud, Sigmund: xxxvi, 60, 65-68
Frost, Robert: 61
Fundamentals: 99

- G -

Gaebelein, Arno Clemens: 93, 94
Galilei, Galileo: 111, 115
Gallup, George Jr.: 75
Gap Theory: 36, 37
Garraty, John A.: 40, 41
Gay, Peter: 144-146
Geocentric: 111, 112, 114-116
Gish, Duane T.: xiii
Gnosticism: 127
Goleman, Daniel: 66
Grecian: 11
Greece: xxi, 11, 52, 107, 109, 110, 119, 120, 122, 123, 133, 142, 147
Greek: xxi, 16, 29, 33, 41, 104, 105, 108, 109, 113, 114, 116, 123, 126, 127, 131, 132, 145
Greek Science: 113, 114, 116
Green, V. H. H.: 130

Gutenberg Press: 136

- H -

Halstead, Beverly: xxxviii
Ham, Ken: 102, 150, 151
Harvard University: xli
Havner, Vance: xxvii
Heliocentric: 112, 115
Henry, Patrick: 44, 45
Heracleitus: 132
Hofstadter, Richard: 92
Holiness: 33, 69, 72-75
Humanist Manifesto: 65
Hummel, Charles E.: 116, 125
Hunter, James Davison: 54-57, 60, 64, 66
Hutton, James: 149
Huxley, Sir Julian: 41

- I -

Industrial Revolution: iv, xxxviii
Iniquity: xviii, xx, xxxv, 143
Instrumentalism: 39

- J -

James, William: 40
Jay, John: 50, 51
Johnston, Henry P.: 51
Jones, Martin-Lloyd: 73

- K -

Kant, Immanual: 146, 146
Kelvin, William Thompson (Lord): 95
Kent, Chancellor James: 8
Kepler, Johannes: 95, 96, 115, 124, 126
Knox, Johannes: 139
Krauthammer, Charles: 121

- L -

LaHaye, Tim: 53, 55
Lamarck, Jean Baptiste: 66
Law of God: xviii
Lewin, Roger: 6
Lindsell, Harold: 7, 10, 12, 139, 146, 148
Linnaeus, Carolus: 95, 115
Lowery, Robert: 68
Lucifer: 29
Lucretius: 109, 110

- M -

Malthus, Thomas: 92
Mar's Hill: 108
Marxism: 39
Maslow, Abraham: 60, 65
Materialism: xiv, xvii, xxxv, 20, 34, 49, 60, 90, 99, 131, 132, 142, 147
Mayflower Compact: 45
McGee, Gordon: 74
Media: xxxiii, 24, 52, 83, 86
Mendel, Gregor: 95, 98

Methodist: xxvii
Middle Ages: 107, 111, 112, 120, 129
Milesian School: 131
Missing Link: xlii
Monoculture: xiv
Moore, John: 83, 96, 97
More, Louis T.: 109
Morison, Samuel: xli
Morris, Henry M.: xi, xiii, xliv, xlv, 11, 66, 68, 71, 95, 96, 98, 109, 110, 131
Mother Nature: 143, 145
Mother Theresa: 57
Muggeridge, Malcolm: 150
Munitz, Milton: 110

- N -

Natural Selection: iv, xxxvi, 18, 36, 41, 98, 134, 135, 148
Naturalism: xvii, 102, 131, 147
Neo-Darwinism: xiv
New Age: 106
Newton, Isaac: xlii, 95, 96, 98, 115, 124, 126
Nimrod: 11, 131
Noah's Flood: xv, 86
North, Gary: 41
Northwest Ordinance: 8

- O -

Olasky, Mervin: 3
Oparin, A. I.: 148
Orians, Gordon H.: 4, 5, 18
Origin of Species: iii, xxxvi, xli, 19, 86, 98-101, 146, 148

Owen, John: 69

- P -

Packer, J. I.: 69
Pantheism: 109, 142
Paradigm: xli, 4-7, 10, 15, 18, 102, 115, 152
Pascal, Blaise: 95, 125, 150
Pasteur, Louis: 95, 98
Peirce, Charles S.: 40
Pentecostal: xxvii
Philosophe: 144
Plato: 113, 114, 127, 133
Polytheism: 10
Popper, Karl: xxxviii
Popoff, Haralan: 57
Preconception: 4
Progress: 12, 37-39, 42, 116
Protagoras: 133
Protestant: 9, 136, 137, 139, 142
Psychology: 34, 36, 42, 52, 65, 66, 69
Ptolemy of Alexander: 112
Public School Curriculum: xxix
Purves, William K.: 4, 5, 18

- R -

Racism: 39
Randolph, Edmund: 50
Reformation: 77, 136, 138-143, 146
Reid, Thomas F.: vi, ix
Relativism: xvii, xxxiv, 38-40, 133, 149

Religion: xvi, xxiv, xxxiii, xlii, 8, 44, 46, 49, 52, 53, 74, 86, 92-94, 115, 116, 121, 129, 135, 136, 142
Renaissance: xxi, xxxix, 90, 99, 102, 105-107, 116, 120, 126-131, 133, 135-139, 141-144, 146
Republic: xlii
Richardson, Alan: 111, 113, 114, 116
Rifkin, Jeremy: 121
Rockefeller, John D.: 39
Rogers, William: 50
Roman Catholic Church: 137
Rome: 52, 92, 111, 116, 120, 122, 139, 141
Roosevelt, Franklin D.: iii
Rousseau, Jean Jacques: 144
Ruin-Reconstruction Theory: 90
Rusk, Roger: x, xvi

- S -

Sagan, Carl: 20, 109, 149
Satan: xviii, xxxv, xxxviii, 11, 99, 106, 131
Schaeffer, Francis A.: 7, 20, 91-94, 102
Schlossberg, Herbert: 3
Scholastics: 127
Sciacca, Fran: 13, 52, 57, 59, 61, 74, 77
Scientific Materialism: xiv, 99
Scientism: i, 146
Scott, Otto: 120, 122
Secular: iv, v, xviii, xxxv, xliv, 11, 12, 34, 64, 66, 105, 108, 129, 133, 137, 139, 141, 144, 153

Self: 13, 33, 39, 41, 52, 53, 56, 58-60, 64, 69, 72, 75-77, 105, 131
Sharp, G. Thomas: 82
Skinner, B. F.: 60, 65
Slusher, Harold S.: xiii
Smith, Wolfgang: 100
Social Darwinism: 39
Social Reform: xlvi
Socialization: xx, xxii, xxxiv, 15, 152
Socrates: 133
Sophists: 133
Spencer, Herbert: 36, 40
Stobart, J. C.: 122
Supreme Court: 50

- T -

Taylor, Gordon R.: 86
Taylor, Ian: xi, 134
Television: ix
Ten Commandments: 42
Thales: 131
Theistic Evolution: 36, 90, 109
Time: ix, xiv, xv, xvii, xviii, xx, xxxiii-xxxv, xlv, 18, 30, 31, 51-52, 58, 73, 75, 83, 84, 87-89, 97-99, 107, 109, 125, 127, 133, 134, 143, 144, 153
Transcendentalism: 40

- U -

UNESCO: See: United Nations Educational Scientific and Cultural Organization
Uniformitarianism: 37, 149

United Nations Educational Scientific and Cultural Organization: 41

- V -

Victorian England: 146
Vine, W.E.: 16
Vitz, Paul C.: 120, 121
Vitz, Paul: 121
Voltaire: 144

- W -

WallBuilders, Inc.: xi
Washington, George: 49, 50, 53
Webster, Hutton: 107, 108, 111, 116, 122, 126
Webster, Noah: 9, 12
Wendt, Herbert: 19
Wesley, Charles & John: 48
Whitcomb, John C.: xiii
White, Errol I.: 101
Whitefield, George: 48
Whitehead, Alfred North: 17, 86
Wilder-Smith, A. E.: xiii, xxii
Williams, Roger: 47
Winthrop, John: 45, 46
Wise, Stephan S.: xvi
Witherspoon, John: 7, 8
World View: ii, v, vi, xiv, xv, xvii, xviii, xx-xxvii, xxxiv, xxxv, xxxviii, xli, xliii-xlvi, 1, 3-5, 7, 8, 11-15, 17-20, 24, 29-35, 51, 52, 56-58, 78, 86-89, 91, 92, 96, 99, 108, 126, 127, 141, 147, 149, 150, 152, 153

World View Transition: 29

- Z -

Zeitgeist: 11
Zeno: 109
Zoroaster: 135

Educate all of your friends, relatives, neighbors, politicians, civic officials, lawyers, school boards, libraries, educators and parents about the attack on our foundation and the much needed repair!

Quantity Prices For
Science According to Moses

Per Single Volume Purchase			
1 copy:	$14.95 each	25 copies:	$12.70 each
6 copies:	$14.20 each	100 copies:	$11.20 each
12 copies:	$13.45 each		

Total Series Purchase			
1 set:	$34.95	25 sets:	$29.70 each
6 sets:	$33.20 each	100 sets:	$26.20 each
12 sets:	$31.45 each		

This book has also been translated and published in the Russian and Spanish languages. It will soon be available in French.

Science According To Moses

Seminars are available to enrich your church, school, convention and workshop. The information in this book, as well as much, much more, is available in live slide-lecture format.

Seminar topics include:

Evolution and the Twentieth Century

Missing Links, Common Ancestors and Other Evolutionary Assumptions

Man: Who is he?

The Origin of Life

Flood Geology: A Scientific Way to View the Earth

DNA Requires An Intelligent Designer

Design: The Evolutionary Nightmare

The Seven Hypotheses of Evolution

The Bible and Modern Science

You can make arrangements for Dr. Sharp or another qualified speaker from Creation Truth Foundation, Inc. to come to your group by simply writing or calling:

Creation Truth Foundation, Inc.
P.O. Box 1435 • Noble, OK 73068
(800) 554-9049   FAX (405) 872-7500

Send me _____ copies of **Science According to Moses**

at _____ per copy, (see previous page for prices).

              TOTAL   _____

Add 20% Postage & Handling,
$2.50 minimum   _____

Oklahoma Residents add 7.5%
            Sales Tax   _____

       GRAND TOTAL   _____

METHOD OF PAYMENT:
☐ Credit Card Orders
☐ Check (make checks payable to: Creation Truth Publications)
☐ Money Order   ☐ Am. Express   ☐ Discover
☐ MasterCard   ☐ Visa

Card No: ☐☐☐☐ • ☐☐☐☐ • ☐☐☐☐ • ☐☐☐☐

☐☐☐☐
Exp. Date   Signature

Mail To:
Creation Truth Publications
P.O. Box 1435 • Noble, OK 73068

Please Print Name and Address:

Name _____

Address _____

City & State _____ Zip _____

CUT ALONG DOTTED LINE